Spices used in curry dishes

PREMILA LAL

INDIAN
cooking for pleasure

HAMLYN

LONDON · NEW YORK · SYDNEY · TORONTO

For my sons, Hemant, Uday, and Rohit
who wanted a book of their own

PHOTOGRAPHER Bryce Atwell
ILLUSTRATOR   Gay John Galsworthy
© Copyright PREMILA LAL 1970
Published by THE HAMLYN PUBLISHING GROUP LTD.
London • New York • Sydney • Toronto
Hamlyn House, Feltham, Middlesex, England
Printed in Czechoslovakia by Svoboda, Prague
T 2120
SBN 600 01996 9

CONTENTS

INTRODUCTION

The growing interest in Indian food, which I noticed recently in Britain, prompted me to write a book on Indian cooking for Western housewives. The preparation of Indian food may at first sight appear complicated and troublesome. This need not be so. In this book I have tried to describe a number of recipes which any reasonably experienced cook should have no difficulty in following. The long drawn out processes used in India are not always practical, suitable or acceptable in Europe. I have therefore ventured to take a few liberties with many old and tried recipes.

Indian food varies from one end of India to the other as do the people, languages and the climate. It is influenced not only by religious, historical and geographical factors but also by the materials available. For example, meat tends to be tough in India and so you will find that all manner of techniques exist for making it tender. (These have influenced the style of cooking as much as the culinary arts of the Moghuls). In the West, meat is more tender so that much of the prolonged cooking, pre-boiling and mincing is unnecessary.

PREMILA LAL

EQUIPMENT USED FOR INDIAN COOKERY

In India a pestle and mortar, or grinding stone and roller, are essential equipment in every kitchen. Spices are usually ground freshly for curries, spiced fish, meat, chicken and vegetables.

In the West a blender or electric grinder can be used instead. I do not always advise the use of these, as quite often the quantities required are small and the waste considerable. It is possible to obtain excellent results by using ready ground spices combined with fresh ginger, garlic, chillis, onions and coriander. The quickest and most efficient way to mince these fresh ingredients finely is by using either a 'Metsaluna' or a 'Zylyss' chopper — the former is better for large quantities, the latter is quicker. If you have neither of these a sharp knife and patience will suffice. A small pestle and mortar is useful for crushing small quantities of spices such as cloves, cardamoms, cinnamon and saffron. No other special equipment is necessary other than that found in most kitchens.

INGREDIENTS USED FOR INDIAN COOKERY

The special techniques which have developed in Indian cooking over the years are, no doubt, the result of a difficult climate. For the greater part of the year it is far too hot to store food, for this reason ingredients have been altered to suit the conditions. Butter is clarified to make ghee which is the desired cooking medium for the greater part of India. Today, because ghee has become expensive, most people use a vegetable ghee (hydrogenated vegetable oil) which is available in Indian and Pakistani grocery shops. Oil is also used in India, particularly in the South and the East. In most of my recipes I have used oil and found it perfectly satisfactory.

In a tropical climate milk turns sour easily so it is made into 'dahi' or yoghurt as it is called here. It is eaten daily in India, by itself; as an ingredient in cooking; or as a tenderiser for meat and chicken. Home made 'dahi' is the best, but it is difficult to make in Britain owing to the cold weather but it can be done.

DAHI OR YOGHURT (1)

To make 'dahi' boil two pints of milk and cool to blood heat. Take five teaspoons of commercial, natural yoghurt and smear it evenly inside a bowl. Pour the milk back and forth from bowl to pan three or four times. Leave undisturbed in a warm place till set — approximately eight hours or overnight, after covering with a clean cloth.
When solidified use as desired.

DAHI OR YOGHURT (2)

Bring 1 pint of milk to the boil and simmer for 1–2 minutes in order to thicken it. Pour into a bowl and set aside to cool to about 106° F — hand-hot temperature — stirring frequently to prevent a skin forming. Then stir in 1 tablespoon of natural yoghurt or yoghurt culture. Pour this mixture immediately into a warm wide-necked vacuum flask, replace the top, and leave undisturbed for 8 hours, when it should be set. Store in the refrigerator.

In all my recipes I have used commercial yoghurt and it is, in most cases, a satisfactory substitute.

Coconut is also used a great deal, particularly in the coastal areas of India. In my recipes I have used either desiccated or creamed coconut, for convenience and speed. If you have plenty of time and coconuts are available, it is worth taking the trouble to make fresh coconut milk which imparts a much better flavour to the food.

To make coconut milk: Grate the flesh of a coconut into a bowl and add one pint of boiling water. Stir and set aside for 30 minutes. Then squeeze and strain the milk through muslin. A second infusion can be made by pouring another pint of boiling water on the coconut. This second infusion will not be as rich as the first but it is quite satisfactory for use in curries.

There are many reputable small shops throughout the country, whose business it is to supply spices. The following grocers in London are well-known stockists.

The Bombay Emporium Ltd. 70 Grafton Way, London, W. 1. Telephone number: 01-387-4514

Harrods Ltd. Kinghtsbridge, London, S. W. 1. Telephone number: 01-730-1234

The Spice Box Bude Street, London, S.W. 1.

All the ingredients mentioned in this book are available either from the big stores and supermarkets or the many Indian and Pakistani grocers' shops. The ground ingredients should be bought in small quantities and kept tightly stoppered in airtight containers. Unless one cooks Indian food every day, no more than two ounces of the *main ingredients*, such as garam masala; ground cummin seeds; ground coriander seeds; turmeric and chilli powder; should be bought. Ground and whole cloves, cardamon and cinnamon should be bought by the half ounce. *Green chillis* are better bought by the ounce, because they quickly dry and lose their flavour, they are best stored in the refrigerator.

Although I have used *green chillis* moderately in these recipes, it is wise to be cautious until you know how hot you like your food to be, begin by halving the recommended number of chillis, for safety.

Coriander leaves can be bought by the bunch, half bunch or as little as you require from Indian, Pakistani and some Greek or Italian greengrocers. They should be used at once because they soon become limp and lose flavour. Coriander is a seasonal herb and is not always in the shops. *Curry leaves*

are usually available, when they are not, bay leaves can be used as a substitute.

While the ground ingredients available in the shops are excellent, you may be tempted to make your own. Home-ground spices have a finer, fresher taste. Here are two curry powder recipes you may wish to try. Use a pestle and mortar or a small electric grinder.

Recipe 1   1 teaspoon *each* fenugreek, mustard and poppy seed

2 teaspoons each cloves, cardamom seeds and dry red chillis

1 tablespoon black peppercorns

1 tablespoon ground ginger

2 tablespoons *each* cummin, coriander seeds and turmeric powder

Grind all the seeds and add the turmeric, then mix with the ground ginger. Sieve, if necessary, and bottle in an airtight jar.

Recipe 2   8 oz. coriander seeds

2 oz. cummin seeds

1 oz. cinnamon

½ oz. cloves

½ oz. black cardamom seeds

1 oz. bay leaves

1 oz. peppercorns

¼ oz. white cardamom seeds

1 nutmeg

¼ oz. mace

Cook all these ingredients in a heavy frying pan (without fat) for 10 minutes. Pound to a fine powder and store in an airtight jar. Use to season all dhal and curry dishes.

Rice Many varieties are available but the most satisfactory for Indian cooking are Basmati and Patna. Both of these can be bought in any good shops.

Dhals (Pulses) The various dhals mentioned in the recipes can be bought at Indian and Pakistani shops. The most common dhal 'masoor' (lentils) and 'matar' (split peas) are available at any grocer.

Tamarind This is the pod of a tropical tree and is used as a souring agent. It is soaked in hot water for 30 minutes and then squeezed and strained. The husk or pod and seeds are discarded and the pulp and water used. For 1 oz. of tamarind, unless otherwise stated, you will need 4 tablespoons of water.

COOKING TIPS

When frying mustard seeds: Cover the pan as the seeds fly all over the place when hot.

When frying ground spices for a curry: After the first minute or so when the mixture becomes very dry and brown, add a few splashes of water then fry again till dry.

When yoghurt is added to a dish: It should be well beaten first and then added a little at a time.

Never use vinegar as a souring agent: Unless it is mentioned specially, as it tends to make the curry bitter.

PLANNING A MEAL

Indian food is very suitable for luncheon or dinner parties because most of the dishes can be prepared in advance and left in the oven or on the hob until the last minute. In India it is usual at a party to serve either a completely vegetarian meal or at least one meat or chicken dish; a fish dish together with one or two vegetable dishes; dhal, rice, roti (bread), yoghurt and one or two pickles or chutneys together with papads.

In Western countries it is sufficient to serve a meat, chicken or fish dish; one or two vegetable dishes with dhal or rice, yoghurt, pickles and papads.

Though it is not common in India to finish the meal with a pudding, a sweet or fruit can be served. Wine is not suitable to serve with Indian food as the flavour is lost when partaken with spiced food. A light lager, on the other hand, is an excellent accompaniment.

Most Indian dishes do not require much garnishing as the traditional way of serving food on a 'thali'* (salver) is very elaborate. (*Illustrated in colour on page 19.*) Three or more small silver or brass bowls, filled with a variety of dishes are placed on a flat matching round 'thali'. A variety of pickles and chutneys are placed on one side with a helping of rice in the centre. Sweetmeats and finely chopped green salad are also put on the 'thali' which add colour to the platter. The only accepted garnishes are finely chopped coriander leaves, crisply fried sliced onion, fried chopped nuts and 'varak' which is very finely beaten silver-leaf.

In Westernised Indian homes there is no rule about garnishing food. It is served on a table laid with crockery and cutlery in the Western style and garnished with salads and fruit as the hostess chooses.

After a meal, 'pan' is served. This is a mixture of finely chopped betel nut, cardamom seeds, aniseed and nuts wrapped in a green leaf, smeared with lime paste; this is chewed and acts as a digestive.

The following menus will give you some idea of
how to plan a meal:

Shahi Murgh
Sabzi Pulao
Behndi Batata
Cuchumber

Nariel Baida Curry
Plain boiled rice
Aloo foogath
Masoor ki dhal
Kela Raitha

Masala Bangra
Dahi Aloo
Palak Paneer
Am raitha
Chapathis

Moghlai Ran
Kichra Pulao
Tamatar curry
Bhendi raita
Bund gobi mircha

WEIGHTS AND MEASURES

Weights throughout the book are given in lb. and oz. Capacity measure in Imperial pints and fractions thereof, with small amounts in spoon measures. For the benefit of American readers liquid ingredients have been given to the nearest U.S. standard cup measure. These follow the English measure i. e. 1 pint (U.S. 2½ cups).

All spoon measures refer to the British Standards Institution specification. All measures are levelled off to the rim of the spoon. To measure fractions of spoons use the small measures provided in measuring sets or divide the level spoon. The American standard measuring spoons are slightly smaller in capacity than the British standard measuring spoons. The proportion however is similar in that 3 American standard teaspoons equal 1 tablespoon. For recipes in this book, use 2 cups U.S. flour for 8 oz. British.

HANDY CONVERSION TABLE

ENGLISH MEASURE	(APPROXIMATE CONVERSION TABLE)	AMERICAN CUPS
1 lb.	Butter or other fat	2 cups
1 lb.	Flour (sifted)	4 cups
1 lb.	Granulated or Castor Sugar	2¼ cups
1 lb.	Brown (moist) Sugar	2¼ cups
1 lb.	Rice	2¼—2½ cups
1 lb.	Dried Fruit (chopped)	2—2½ cups
1 lb.	Raw Chopped Meat (finely packed)	2 cups
1 lb.	Lentils or Split Peas	2 cups
1 lb.	Dry Breadcrumbs	4 cups
8 oz.	Butter or Margarine	1 cup
8 oz.	Lard	1 cup
7 oz.	Castor Sugar	1 cup
7 oz.	Soft Brown Sugar	1 cup (packed)
6⅓ oz.	Chopped Dates	1 cup
5 oz.	Currants	1 cup
5½ oz.	Cooked Rice	1 cup
5¾ oz.	Seedless Raisins	1 cup
5 oz.	Candied Peel	1 cup
5 oz.	Chopped Mixed Nuts	1 cup
5 oz.	Sliced Apple	1 cup
2½ oz.	Desiccated Coconut	1 cup
2 oz.	Fresh Breadcrumbs	1 cup
¼ oz.	Dried Yeast	1 packet

ENGLISH MEASURE		AMERICAN CUPS
¼ oz.	Gelatine	1 tablespoon
¾ tablespoon	Gelatine	1 envelope
½ oz.	Flour	1 level tablespoon*
1 oz.	Flour	2 level tablespoons
1 oz.	Sugar	1 level tablespoon
½ oz.	Butter	1 level tablespoon smoothed off
1 oz.	Jam or Jelly	1 level tablespoon

* must be standard U.S. measuring tablespoon

METRIC EQUIVALENTS

It is difficult to convert to French measures with absolute accuracy, but 1 oz. is equal to approximately 30 grammes, 2 lb. 3 oz. to 1 kilogramme. For liquid measure, approximately 1¾

English pints may be regarded as equal to 1 litre; ½ pint to 3 decilitres (scant); 3½ fluid oz. to 1 decilitre.

OVEN TEMPERATURES

DESCRIPTION OF OVEN	APPROXIMATE TEMPERATURE CENTRE OF OVEN °F	THERMOSTAT SETTING
Very Slow or Very Cool	200—250	¼ = 240 ½ = 265 1 = 290
Slow or Cool	250—300	2 = 310
Very Moderate	300—350	3 = 335
Moderate	350—375	4 = 350
Moderately Hot		5 = 375
to Hot	375—400	6 = 400
Hot to Very Hot	425—450	7 = 425
Very Hot	450—500	8 = 450
		9 = 470

RICE

Rice is the staple food of South, Central and East India and is eaten on festive occasions in the North. It is most commonly eaten plain boiled, but on occasions it is cooked with spices added to vegetables, meat, chicken or fish to make a variety of pulaos and biryanis. Rice is delicious when cooked well. A little care taken in the purchase and preparation is all that is needed to achieve success. Patna and Basmati rice are considered to have the best flavours, but other long grain types may be substituted. However, if the rice is highly refined, the instructions on the pack, not the ones given below, should be followed. Usually 2 oz. of rice per head is ample in Europe. An **extra** 2 oz. may be added 'for the table' if heavy eaters are expected. The rice must be cleaned carefully to remove any pieces of husk which may be present. Wash thoroughly by placing rice in a saucepan under running, cold water. Swish around the pan two or three times then leave it under a light flow until the water in the pan is quite clear.

Leave the rice to soak for at least 30 minutes but the longer it soaks the quicker it cooks. To boil 8 oz. of rice you will need just under 1 pint of water (U.S. 2¼ cups), (a little less if the rice has been soaking for a long time). Put the rice and cold water, well seasoned with salt, on the hob at the fastest heat and when it is well and truly boiling, cover with a tight-fitting lid and turn down the heat to low. In my experience, when using an electric cooker, once the rice comes to the boil, the hot place can be turned off and within 10—15 minutes the pan is uncovered and the rice is cooked to perfection — dry, with each grain separate. If by chance, the rice is sticky, place it in an oven-proof dish, cover lightly with foil and let it dry out in a moderate oven before serving. Another way of boiling rice is to clean, wash and soak 8 oz. rice as described above, then bring 3 pints (U.S. 7½ cups) of salted water to the boil in a big saucepan, drain and add the rice, stir once then let it boil for about 15—20 minutes. Always test to see if rice is cooked. When tender strain the rice through a colander and pour 4 tablespoons cold water over it. Drain thoroughly before serving. This method is very successful but the previous one is preferable because the rice retains all its food value. Pulaos and biryanis are good party dishes as they can be prepared earlier in the day, covered with foil and put in a moderate oven 30—35 minutes before serving.

SABZI PULAO

MIXED VEGETABLE PULAO

Preparation time 15 minutes
Cooking time 1 hour
To serve 4

You will need

8 oz. Patna or Basmati rice
¾ pint (U.S. 2 cups) water, salted
2 large onions
4 oz. carrots
1 small aubergine
1 green pepper
2 ripe tomatoes
8 oz. cauliflower
oil for shallow frying
6 oz. shelled peas
¼ teaspoon garam masala
¼ teaspoon saffron, crushed
½ teaspoon chilli powder
4 cloves
1-inch piece cinnamon
salt to taste

Wash the rice thoroughly under cold running water until the water runs clear. Cover the rice with the water and par-boil. Drain and set aside. Slice the onions, carrots, aubergine and green pepper; quarter the tomatoes then break the cauliflower into small flowerets. Heat some oil in a pan and fry the onions until slightly brown. Add the peas, carrots and tomatoes and simmer on a low heat for 15 minutes. Add the aubergine, green pepper, tomatoes, cauliflower, garam masala, saffron, chilli powder, cloves and cinnamon. Simmer for another 15 minutes or until all the vegetables are cooked. Season with salt. Using a large casserole dish cover the bottom with half the cooked vegetables, then a layer of half the rice. Another layer of vegetables and rice topped with a last layer of vegetables. Cover with foil and bake in a moderate oven (350° F. — Gas Mark 4) for 20 minutes.

Mixed vegetable pulao

SABZI PULAO

VEGETABLE PULAO 2

Preparation time 15 minutes
Cooking time 40 minutes
To serve 4

You will need

8 oz. Patna or Basmati rice
4 medium carrots
2 medium-sized onions
oil for frying
4 cloves
2 whole cardamom seeds
2 sticks cinnamon
1 teaspoon whole cummin
  or caraway seeds
6 oz. shelled peas
1 pint (U.S. 2½ cups) chicken stock
  or water
salt to taste

Wash the rice well and leave aside with enough water to cover. Slice the carrots into rounds; slice onions. Heat some oil in a heavy saucepan and fry cloves, cardamoms, cummin seeds and cinnamon for a minute. Add onions, peas and carrots and fry for five minutes. Drain the rice and add and fry for another five minutes. Pour in the stock, season with salt and cook uncovered for 15 minutes. Remove and cover and finish cooking in a moderate oven, (350° F. — Gas Mark 4) for another 15 minutes.

ANDA PULAO

EGG PULAO

Preparation time   5 minutes
Cooking time   35 minutes
To serve   4

You will need

8 oz. Patna or Basmati rice
1 onion
2 tablespoons sultanas
2-inch stick cinnamon
4 cloves
2 cardamoms
salt to taste
6 hard-boiled eggs
oil for frying

Wash and soak the rice in water. Slice onion and fry till lightly brown. Add sultanas, cinnamon, cloves and cardamoms and fry for a minute. Drain rice and add, fry for five minutes. Pour in almost one pint water. Season with salt and cook till rice is almost tender. Meanwhile fry two of the hard-boiled eggs in a little oil till lightly brown. Slice and put carefully into the rice. Place in a hot oven, (400° F — Gas Mark 6) for 10 minutes to dry. Slice the remaining eggs and arrange on top of the rice.

Egg pulao

Cauliflower pulao

GOBI PULAO

CAULIFLOWER PULAO

Preparation time   10 minutes
Cooking time   40 minutes
To serve   4

You will need

8 oz. Patna or Basmati rice
8 oz. cauliflower
1 onion
oil for frying
1 teaspoon whole cummin
  or caraway seeds
scant pint (U.S. 2¼ cups) water
½ teaspoon turmeric powder
salt to taste

Wash and soak rice in water for 30 minutes. Meanwhile, cut cauliflower into sprigs and slice onion finely. Fry the cauliflower in a little oil till nearly cooked and lightly brown. Drain and keep aside. Fry the cummin seeds for a minute or two till reddish-brown. Add onion and fry till brown. Drain rice and add to the spices, fry gently for three minutes then add the water, turmeric and salt. Cook for five minutes, stir gently, then add the cauliflower. Cover and leave to cook till the water has evaporated and the rice is cooked. Serve with raw onion and cucumber salad.

MUTANJAN

LAMB AND LEMON RICE

Preparation time 15 minutes
Cooking time 1½ hours
To serve 4

You will need

1 lb. lamb, boned
1 large onion
1-inch fresh root ginger
2 teaspoons coriander seeds
3 × 1-inch sticks cinnamon
pinch of salt
½ pint (U.S. 1¼ cups) water
2 oz. granulated sugar
juice of 2 lemons
8 oz. Patna or Basmati rice
scant pint (U.S. 2¼ cups) water
1½ oz. butter
6 cloves
12 peppercorns
12 cardamoms
20 almonds
¾ teaspoon saffron, soaked in
    1 tablespoon warm milk

Cut lamb into 1-inch cubes, cut onion in quarters, chop ginger. Put meat in a saucepan with the onion. Tie the ginger, coriander seeds and cinna-

Prawn pulao

mon in a piece of muslin and add to the meat. Add salt and water. Simmer until the meat is tender and the liquid reduced by half.
The meat should simmer very slowly for at least one hour. Remove the muslin and squeeze to draw out the flavour. Add the sugar and juice of 1½ lemons to the meat in the pan. Cook slowly until a thin syrup forms. Parboil the rice in the water and juice of remaining ½ lemon. Drain thoroughly. Melt 1½ oz. butter in a saucepan, add the coarsely-crushed peppercorns and cardamoms. Fry for 1—2 minutes before adding the meat and rice to the pan. Blanch, peel and quarter the almonds. Add along with the saffron. Cook gently until the liquid is completely absorbed and the rice is cooked.

JINGA PULAO

PRAWN PULAO

Preparation time 10 minutes
Cooking time 40 minutes
To serve 4

You will need

8 oz. Patna or Basmati rice
1 pint peeled prawns
½ teaspoon chilli powder
pinch of salt
1 teaspoon turmeric powder
1 large onion
oil for frying
1 teaspoon whole cummin seeds
2 cardamoms
1-inch stick cinnamon
3 cloves
1 pint (U.S. 2½ cups) chicken or fish stock
    or water

Wash the rice and soak in water. Clean prawns and rub with chilli powder, salt and turmeric. Chop onion. Heat some oil and fry the prawns till golden brown. Remove and keep aside. In the same pan fry onion, cummin seeds, cinnamon, cloves and cardamoms, for ten minutes. Drain the rice and add to the onions. Fry for five minutes, pour in stock, season and cook covered until all liquid is absorbed and rice cooked. Just before the rice is cooked add the fried prawns.

RILLA PULAO

SPICED LAMB PULAO

Preparation time   30 minutes
Cooking time   1 hour
To serve   4

You will need

8 oz. Patna or Basmati rice
1 lb. lean lamb
3 onions
1 green chilli
oil for frying
scant pint (U.S. 2¼ cups) boiling water

FOR MASALA PASTE

2 green chillis
bunch coriander leaves
1-inch fresh root ginger
sprig mint leaves
1 teaspoon powdered cummin seeds
1 teaspoon pepper
½ teaspoon turmeric powder
½ teaspoon ground cloves
1 teaspoon garam masala
salt to taste

Wash rice and soak in water. Trim lamb and cut into cubes. Chop onions and chilli. Now prepare the ingredients for the masala paste. Finely grate or mince the chillis, coriander leaves, ginger and mint together. Mix with the cummin, pepper, turmeric, cloves and garam masala, to make a paste. Heat some oil in a large pan and fry the sliced onions and green chilli until golden brown. Add the lamb. Fry for 10 minutes before adding a little of the water to prevent the meat from sticking to the bottom of the pan. Cook very gently until lamb is tender. Add the masala paste and season with salt. Fry for 10 minutes. Drain the rice and add, fry for 2—3 minutes. Add the boiling water and cook very gently until all the liquid is absorbed and the rice cooked. Serve with a crisp salad.

Lamb and lemon rice

AM PULAO

MANGO PULAO

Preparation time   10 minutes
Cooking time   20 minutes
To serve   4

You will need

8 oz. Patna or Basmati rice
scant pint (U.S. 2¼ cups) boiling water
salt to taste
½ teaspoon turmeric powder
2 half-ripe mangoes
2 teaspoons ground cummin seeds
1½ teaspoons chilli powder
4 oz. grated coconut
2 oz. butter
1 oz. gram dhal
1 sprig curry leaves
  or 2 bay leaves
1 tablespoon mustard seeds

Wash the rice thoroughly and put to boil in a scant pint of water with salt and turmeric. Peel and slice the mangoes and mix with the cummin seeds, chilli powder and grated coconut. Fry the dhal, curry leaves and mustard seeds in 1 oz. of the butter and add to the rice. When the rice is almost cooked, stew the mango in the remaining butter.
Put the rice in a serving dish and arrange the mango on top. Serve with sweet chutney.

Mango pulao

AM CHAWAL

MANGO RICE

Preparation time   10 minutes
Cooking time   25—30 minutes
To serve   4

You will need

8 oz. rice
scant pint (U.S. 2¼ cups) salted water
2 tablespoons oil
1 large raw mango
  or 2 cooking apples
2 teaspoons gram dhal, soaked for 1 hour
1 teaspoon chilli powder
pinch dry mustard
½ teaspoon turmeric powder
pinch of asafoetida
2 dry red chillis
2 bay leaves

Wash the rice thoroughly and soak for 30 minutes. Boil in salted water until tender but firm. Drain and stir in one tablespoon of the oil lightly with a fork so that the grains remain separate. Now peel the mango or apples, cut into thin wedges mix with rice. Heat remaining oil in a pan, drain and lightly brown the dhal. Add the ground spices and fry well for five minutes. Add the chillis and bay leaves and fry for one minute. Mix well with the rice, cover with a close-fitting lid and leave on a very low heat until serving time.

KICHRA PULAO

MIXED LENTIL PULAO

Preparation time   20 minutes
Cooking time   1½ hours
To serve   4

You will need

8 oz. Basmati or Patna rice
1 oz. each of yellow masoor and
  gram dhal
salt to taste
¼ teaspoon turmeric powder

FOR MASALA PASTE

1 green chilli
1 clove garlic
1-inch fresh root ginger
1-inch stick cinnamon
6 peppercorns
4 cloves

1 large potato
1 large carrot
oil for frying
8 oz. onions
2 large tomatoes
1½ lb. stewing steak
1 teaspoon ground coriander seeds
½ teaspoon ground cummin seeds
1 teaspoon chilli powder
4 oz. cooked peas
¼ pint (U.S. ⅔ cup) stock

Wash rice and dhal thoroughly, soak for 30 minutes then par-boil and drain. Add salt and turmeric. Finely mince or grate the green chilli, garlic and ginger. Crush the cinnamon, peppercorns and cloves. Dice the potato and carrots; fry them in a little oil until tender. Set aside. Slice the onions, chop tomatoes and cut steak into cubes. Fry the onion until golden brown add the tomatoes and then the steak. Stir well and add all the spices and cook for 1¼ hours or until the meat is almost done. Put the cooked vegetables and meat at the bottom of a large saucepan, cover with the rice and dhal. Add stock, cover with a tightfitting lid and simmer for the remainder of the time or until rice is tender.

KITCHEREE

RICE WITH LENTILS

Preparation time 5 minutes
Cooking time 40 minutes
To serve 4

You will need

8 oz. rice
4 oz. yellow moong dhal
1½ oz. butter
1 onion, chopped
½ teaspoon crushed garlic
½-inch fresh root ginger, finely sliced
4 cloves
2-inch stick of cinnamon
4 cardamoms
½ teaspoon peppercorns
1 teaspoon turmeric powder
salt to taste
2 tablespoons milk

FOR THE GARNISH

slices of hard-boiled egg
fried onion slices

Mix the rice and dhal together, wash thoroughly and soak in fresh water for one hour. Meanwhile, fry the onion, garlic, ginger and other spices, except the turmeric and salt in the butter, until the

onions are tender. Drain the rice and dhal and add to the onion. Sprinkle with turmeric and salt and toss lightly. Cook very gently for five minutes. Add boiling water to come ½ inch above the rice. Cover the pan with a tightly fitting lid and simmer gently until all the moisture is absorbed and the rice cooked. Before serving, sprinkle the rice with milk. Garnish with egg and onion slices.

MASALA KITCHEREE

SPICED PEAS AND RICE

Preparation time 15 minutes
Cooking time 50 minutes
To serve 4

You will need

8 oz. rice
1 large onion
1 green chilli
½-inch fresh root ginger
1 clove garlic
2 boiled potatoes
oil for frying
½ teaspoon garam masala
½ teaspoon cummin seeds
½ teaspoon turmeric powder
pinch of chilli powder
½ tablespoon desiccated coconut, soaked in
  2 tablespoons hot water
4 tablespoon peas
salt to taste
1 teaspoon chopped coriander leaves

Wash the rice thoroughly in running water until the water runs clear. Set aside. Chop the onion and green chilli finely. Chop the piece of ginger and garlic clove. Cube the potatoes. Fry onion in some oil and when light brown add the ginger, garlic and green chilli. Fry for two minutes and then add the garam masala together with the cummin seeds, turmeric, chilli powder and coconut. Fry for 10 minutes. Add the drained rice and peas and fry until slightly brown. Add the potatoes and salt and cover with enough water to come ¾ inch above the rice. When water begins to boil, lower heat; cover and simmer until the rice is done and water evaporated. Sprinkle coriander leaves on top before serving.

Rice with lentils

Traditional Thali dinner

Whole Bengal beans

KABLI CHANNA

WHOLE BENGAL BEANS

Illustrated in colour on opposite page

Preparation time   15 minutes
Cooking time   1 hour
To serve   4

You will need

8 oz. Kabli channas
generous pint (U.S. 2¾ cups) of water
pinch of salt
1 onion
2-inch piece fresh root ginger
2 cloves garlic
2 chillis
2 tomatoes
oil for frying
2 teaspoons ground coriander seeds
½ teaspoon ground cummin seeds
½ teaspoon chilli powder
4 cloves
1-inch stick cinnamon
juice of 1 lemon
1 tablespoon fresh coriander leaves, chopped

Wash and soak the channas overnight in the water. Then add salt and cook gently until the channas are soft and almost splitting (approximately 30–45 minutes). Meanwhile slice the onion finely, mince the ginger and garlic finely, slit the chillis and chop the tomatoes. Heat some oil in a saucepan and fry the onions until golden brown. Add the ginger and garlic and fry well. Now add the ground coriander, cummin seeds and chilli powder. Fry well and if too dry sprinkle with a little water. When well fried add tomatoes and chillis and fry for 10 minutes. Add the drained, cooked channas and cook gently for 10 minutes before adding the water in which the channas were cooked. Simmer for 25 minutes. Add lemon juice 15 minutes before the end of the cooking time. Garnish with chopped coriander leaves.

TAMATAR CHAWAL

TOMATO RICE

Preparation time   10 minutes
Cooking time   45 minutes
To serve   4

You will need

8 oz. Basmati rice
1 lb. tomatoes
oil for frying
1 large onion, sliced
1 clove garlic, crushed
1-inch fresh root ginger, finely chopped
½ teaspoon black pepper, freshly ground
4 cloves
salt to taste
water

FOR THE GARNISH

¼ bunch fresh coriander leaves, chopped

Wash rice and soak for at least 30 minutes. Cook tomatoes in water for five minutes, then skin and sieve. Heat some oil in a saucepan and fry onions till brown. Add the spices and salt. Fry well for five minutes. Add rice and fry for a few more minutes. Make up tomato juice to a scant pint (U.S. 2¼ cups) with water and add to the rice. Bring to the boil, cover, and simmer gently till rice is tender and liquid absorbed. Garnish with chopped coriander leaves.

SOOKHI DHAL

DRY LENTILS

Preparation time   5 minutes
Cooking time   40 minutes
To serve   4

You will need

8 oz. black gram dhal
2 cloves garlic
2 green chillis
oil for frying
1 teaspoon turmeric powder
1 teaspoon powdered cummin seeds
salt to taste
a little water

Soak dhal for 1 hour in water. Mince garlic and chillis. Heat oil in a pan. Fry garlic, chillis, turmeric and cummin seeds for three minutes. Drain dhal and add to spices. Fry for five minutes. Add salt and water, cover and cook gently till tender and dry.

CELERY SAMBAR

CELERY WITH LENTILS

Preparation time   15 minutes
Cooking time   35 minutes
To serve   4

You will need

8 oz. dhal
1 pint (U.S. 2½ cups) water
3 stalks celery
½ teaspoon turmeric powder
½-inch slice of creamed coconut
½ teaspoon chilli powder
1 teaspoon ground cummin seeds
salt to taste
oil for frying
pinch of asafoetida (optional)
1 rounded teaspoon mustard seeds

Wash the dhal thoroughly. Cover with 1 pint of water and cook until tender adding more water if necessary. Wash, trim and cut the celery into 4-inch pieces. Simmer in a little water with the turmeric until tender. Add the celery, coconut, chilli powder, cummin seeds and salt to the dhal. Heat some oil in a frying pan and fry the asafoetida, if used, with the mustard seeds, until they crackle. Combine with the dhal and serve with plain boiled rice.

MASOOR KI DHAL

SPICED LENTILS

Preparation time   5 minutes
Cooking time   1 hour
To serve   4

You will need

8 oz. Masoor dhal
1 pint (U.S. 2½ cups) salted water
oil for frying
1 teaspoon mustard seeds
2 green chillis, sliced
1 onion' sliced
1 clove garlic, crushed
½ teaspoon turmeric powder
salt to taste

Wash dhal thoroughly and leave to soak for 30 minutes. Drain and place into a saucepan with the water. Bring to the boil; cover and reduce the heat. Simmer very gently, stirring occasionally until soft and creamy. Add more water, if necessary. Heat some oil in a small frying pan and fry the mustard seeds till they crackle. Add chillis, onion and garlic and fry well till onion begins to brown. Add to dhal with the turmeric and mix to combine before serving.

BADSHAKI KITCHEREE

SPICED RICE WITH LENTILS

Preparation time   10 minutes
Cooking time   35 minutes
To serve   4

You will need

8 oz. Patna or Basmati rice
4 oz. yellow dhal
4 oz. potato
4 oz. onions
1 pint (U.S. 2½ cups) water
salt to taste
oil for frying
2 oz. each currants, pistachios, almonds
pinch of chilli powder
½ teaspoon ground coriander seeds
½ teaspoon ground cummin seeds
sprig curry leaves
    or 2 bay leaves
2 green chillis
2 1-inch sticks cinnamon

Wash rice and dhal well in running water. Soak separately for at least 30 minutes. Meanwhile cube potato and slice onions. Now boil the rice in the water for five minutes before adding the dhal, add salt and cook gently till done adding more water if necessary. Fry half the onions and all the potatoes and add to the rice. Lightly fry the currants and nuts and add them too. Add the chilli powder, coriander and cummin. Stir well and remove from the heat. Fry the rest of the onions, curry leaves and chopped green chillis and add to the rice. Put in the cinnamon and replace the pan on a low heat and cook for a further five minutes.

KHUTTI DHAL

SOUR LENTILS

Preparation time 15 minutes
Cooking time 1 hour
To serve 4

You will need

8 oz. dhal
¾ pint (U.S. 2 cups) water
ghee or oil for frying
1 medium-sized onion, sliced
2 oz. tamarind, soaked in
  ¼ pint (U.S. ⅔ cup) hot water

FOR THE MASALA

2 cloves of garlic, crushed
4 cardamoms, crushed
¼ teaspoon ground cloves
½ teaspoon garam masala
½ teaspoon chilli powder
1 dessertspoon coriander leaves
salt to taste

Squeeze the tamarind, discard the husk; use only the water.
Wash the dhal thoroughly. Boil in the water until cooked. Heat some ghee or oil in a frying pan and fry the onion until brown. Combine the masala ingredients. Add the tamarind water, along with the masala ingredients to the onion. Mix into the dhal and cook for a further 15 minutes.

KOOTU

MIXED VEGETABLES AND LENTILS

Preparation time 15 minutes
Cooking time 30 minutes
To serve 4

You will need

1 lb. mixed vegetables (yam, gourds, beans,
  carrots, cauliflower etc.)
4 oz. yellow dhal
¼ teaspoon freshly ground pepper
1 teaspoon turmeric powder
salt to taste
½-inch slice of creamed coconut
1 teaspoon molasses
oil for frying
1 teaspoon mustard seeds
2 red chillis
2 curry leaves *or* bay leaves

Chop the vegetables into small pieces. Wash the dhal thoroughly. Put the dhal and vegetables in a pan together and barely cover with water. Simmer gently until cooked. Season with pepper, turmeric and salt. Add coconut and cook for a further 10 minutes. Remove from the heat and add molasses. In another pan fry the mustard seeds, chillis and curry leaves for a few minutes. Add to the vegetables, mix well and serve with plain boiled rice.

Mixed vegetables and lentils

ORIENTAL BIRYANI

SAVOURY MEAT RICE

Preparation time 15 minutes
Cooking time 1 hour 45 minutes
To serve 4

You will need

8 oz. Patna or Basmati rice
½ teaspoon garlic powder
½ teaspoon ground cinnamon
½ teaspoon ground cardamom seeds
1 teaspoon turmeric powder
water to mix
1 lb. lamb or beef
1 large onion, sliced
1 carton yoghurt
ghee or oil for frying
salt to taste
4 oz. potatoes
1 oz. butter, melted
pinch of saffron (optional)

Wash rice thoroughly in running water. Boil, drain and keep aside. Mix the garlic powder, cinnamon, cardamons and turmeric together with a little water to make a paste. Cut the meat into large cubes; slice the onion and beat the yoghurt. Put the meat into a saucepan with a little ghee or oil, add the spice-paste, onion, yoghurt and salt and cook until the meat is tender and the gravy very thick and reduced. Cut the potatoes into cubes and fry in a little oil until cooked. Set aside. Now take a large casserole put in a little melted butter and add the saffron. Put in the rice, meat and potatoes in layers until all are used up. Finally, brush the top with a little more melted butter and brown in a hot oven, (400° F. — Gas Mark 6). Do not keep uncovered in the oven for too long. If you cannot serve immediately cover with foil and reduce the heat.

SEVIAN PULAU

VERMICELLI PULAO

Preparation time 15 minutes
Cooking time 1 hour
To serve 4-6

You will need

4 potatoes
2 oz. cashew nuts
oil for frying
12 oz. vermicelli
1 teaspoon mustard seeds
2 large onions, finely sliced
2 tablespoons gram flour
1½ pints (U.S. 3¾ cups) water
1 teaspoon chilli powder
2 teaspoons ground coriander seeds
½ teaspoon ground cinnamon
2 bay leaves
salt to taste

Boil the potatoes in their skins, peel and cut them into 1-inch cubes. Chop cashew nuts and fry in oil until golden. Drain and set aside. In the same pan fry the vermicelli until golden, then drain and set aside. Fry the mustard seeds and, when spluttering, add the onions and fry for five minutes. Stir in the flour, add the water and bring to the boil. Add potatoes, vermicelli, cashew nuts, spices, bay leaves and salt. Stir and simmer till the vermicelli is cooked and water evaporated. Remove from the heat and serve after five minutes.

JINGA BIRYANI

CURRIED RICE WITH PRAWNS

Preparation time 15 minutes
Cooking time 40 minutes
To serve 4

You will need

8 oz. Patna or Basmati rice
2 large onions
1-inch fresh root ginger
2 cloves garlic
8 oz. tomatoes
oil for frying
2 pints peeled prawns
1 teaspoon ground cummin seeds
1 teaspoon garam masala
½ teaspoon chilli powder
1 teaspoon turmeric powder
few curry *or* bayleaves
salt to taste
1 pint (U.S. 2½ cups) fish stock *or* water

Wash the rice and soak in water. Mince the onions, ginger and garlic together; chop tomatoes. Heat some oil in a heavy saucepan and fry the onions, ginger and garlic for seven minutes, add prawns, cummin, garam masala, chilli powder and turmeric and curry or bayleaves. Fry for two minutes. Add tomatoes, season with salt and cook for 15 minutes on medium heat, stirring occasionally. Drain rice and add, fry for three minutes and pour in stock. Cook on a low heat till liquid is absorbed and rice tender.

MUTTON BIRYANI

RICE WITH LAMB

Preparation time   20 minutes
Cooking time   2½ hours
To serve   4

You will need

1 lb. lean lamb
½-inch fresh root ginger
½ teaspoon chilli powder
½ teaspoon ground cinnamon
½ teaspoon ground cloves
½ teaspoon ground cardamom seeds
1 teaspoon turmeric powder
1 carton yoghurt
8 oz. onions
8 oz. potatoes
8 oz. Patna or Basmati rice
oil for frying
salt to taste
½ teaspoon saffron, soaked in
  1 tablespoon water
melted butter

Cut lamb into pieces. Mince the ginger very finely. Put lamb into a bowl with all the spices and yoghurt, mix well and set aside to marinade for three hours. Now slice the onions and peel and cube the potatoes. Wash the rice thoroughly and leave to soak for 30 minutes. Fry the onions in a little oil until crisp. Fry the potatoes separately, season with salt. Par-boil the rice and drain. Put three-quarters of the rice into a heavy pan. Reserve a few onion slices for garnish and arrange the remainder with the meat and potatoes on top. Cover with the remaining rice. Decorate the top with the rest of the

onions then add the saffron and a little melted butter. Cover the pan making it completely air-tight by putting foil under the lid. Place on a very low heat for about 2 hours or cook in a cool oven, (300 °F — Gas Mark 2) for the same length of time.

KUTCHI BIRYANI

SPICED RICE WITH LAMB

Preparation time   30 minutes
Cooking time   1 hour 10 minutes
To serve   4

You will need

8 oz. Patna or Basmati rice
1 lb. lamb
1 carton yoghurt
2 large onions
3 cloves garlic
1-inch fresh root ginger
2 dry red chillis
½ teaspoon saffron
oil for frying
salt
2 cardamoms
1 teaspoon cummin seeds
1 stick cinnamon
4 cloves
scant pint (U.S. 2¼ cups) of boiling water
½ teaspoon saffron

FOR THE GARNISH

Deep fried onion rings

Wash and soak the rice in water for at least 30 minutes. Cut the meat into cubes, and soak in yoghurt for 20 minutes. Slice onions, crush garlic, mince ginger and chillis; crush saffron. Heat some oil in a saucepan and fry onions till golden brown. Add the meat and yoghurt together with all the spices except the saffron. Fry until the meat is brown, turn down the heat and cook gently until the meat is tender. Drain rice and add to the meat. Fry until brown then add water. Cover and when the rice is almost cooked add the saffron. Garnish with fried onion rings.

Minced beef with peas

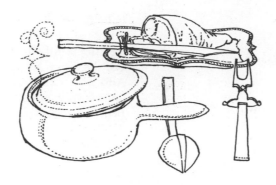

MEAT

Meat is usually eaten in North India, although it is not unknown in the South. Goat is the most commonly available meat; mutton and lamb are rare; and beef is never cooked or eaten in a Hindu household although it is available in some large cities. In the recipes that follow I have substituted lamb for the mutton of the original recipes. In some recipes where minced lamb is called for, minced beef or veal can be used instead.

Meat is cooked in many ways and curry is only one of them. The recipes for curry are legion. From the North come the tandoori dishes (cooked in a tandoor or clay oven) in which Moghul influence is evident from the choice of spices and the methods of cooking. From the North also, come the kababs, made of minced meat or pieces of meat. These are often marinated in yoghurt, threaded on to a skewer and cooked over a charcoal fire. From the coastal areas of West and South India the distinctive flavour of coconut can be tasted in all meat dishes and curries.

Meat in Britain, usually tender, does not require as much cooking as the meat in India and I have modified all the recipes accordingly. When lamb is required in a recipe, either for kababs or curry, it is preferable to buy the leg and not the shoulder as leg of lamb is less fat.

Stewing steak can be used for curries but if at all tough, increase the cooking time. The gravy of a curry should be thick — never watery. Where water is called for in a recipe be sparing in its use, more can always be added later.

KHEEMA MATAR

MINCED BEEF WITH PEAS

Preparation time   15 minutes
Cooking time   45 minutes
To serve   4

You will need

1 onion
4 tomatoes
oil for frying
2 cloves garlic
½-inch fresh root ginger
1 lb. minced lean beef
½ teaspoon turmeric powder
½ teaspoon garam masala
½ teaspoon chilli powder
1 teaspoon ground coriander
8 oz. shelled peas
salt to taste

Chop onion finely and peel and chop tomatoes. Heat some oil and fry onion for three minutes. Crush the garlic and finely mince the ginger and add to the onions and fry for two minutes. Put in meat and fry till dry and brown. Add tomatoes, spices, peas, salt and a little water and simmer for 20 minutes until all the liquid has been absorbed and the peas and meat are tender.

MOGHLAI KOFTAS

STUFFED MEAT BALLS

Preparation time 30 minutes
Cooking time 1 hour 40 minutes
To serve 4

You will need

FOR THE FILLING

1 hard-boiled egg
1 potato
2 dried apricots
oil for frying
1 dessertspoon desiccated coconut, soaked in
  2 dessertspoons milk
1 teaspoon each of poppy and sesame seeds

FOR THE KOFTAS

1 lb. minced beef
2 slices white bread, grated
1 teaspoon freshly ground pepper
1-inch fresh root ginger, finely minced
2 cloves garlic, crushed
2 green chillis, finely minced
pinch of salt
1 egg
oil for frying

FOR THE GRAVY

oil or ghee for frying
2 onions, finely chopped
2-inch stick of cinnamon
2 cardamom seeds
2 cloves
1 clove garlic, crushed
½-inch fresh root ginger, minced finely
1 green chilli, finely minced
1 teaspoon chilli powder
2 cartons yoghurt
1 oz. raisins
1 oz. split almonds
salt to taste

Chop hard-boiled egg, potato and apricots into very small pieces. Fry chopped ingredients in a little oil together with the remaining ingredients for the filling, set aside.
For the koftas, mix meat well with breadcrumbs, pepper, ginger, garlic, chillis, salt and egg. Divide mixture into 8 portions. Shape each portion into a ball, flatten in the palm of the hand and place a little of the filling in the centre. Close on all sides forming into balls and fry.
For the gravy, fry onions in oil or ghee until brown. Add the cinnamon, cardamoms, cloves, garlic, ginger, chilli and chilli powder. Fry for 10 minutes. Beat the yoghurt, add to the gravy and simmer for 35 minutes. Season and add the fried koftas, raisins and almonds. Cook gently for a further 20 minutes.

KHEEMA

CURRIED MINCED BEEF

Preparation time 15 minutes
Cooking time 50 minutes
To serve 4

You will need

6 onions
1 lb. leeks
oil for frying
1 teaspoon turmeric powder
2 teaspoons chilli powder
1 lb. minced beef
salt to taste
6 hard-boiled eggs, finely chopped

Slice onions, wash and mince or chop leeks finely. Put some oil in a pan and fry the onions till slightly

Stuffed aubergines

Minced lamb with cabbage

brown. Add the turmeric and when the raw smell
has evaporated put in the chilli powder. Fry to
brown and then add the meat, leeks and salt. Gently
cook, covered, for 30 minutes. If very dry add a
little water. Remove the lid and stir in the eggs.
Serve at once.

KHEEMA BAINGAN

STUFFED AUBERGINES

Preparation time 10 minutes
Cooking time 1 hour 10 minutes
To serve 4

You will need

1 large onion
oil for frying
12 oz. minced beef
2 tomatoes
1 teaspoon ground coriander seeds
½ teaspoon chilli powder
1 teaspoon garam masala
¼ teaspoon turmeric powder
¼ teaspoon ground ginger
salt to taste
4 medium-sized aubergines

Chop onion and fry till light brown, add the meat
and fry till dry. Chop the tomatoes and add with

the spices to the meat. Lower the heat and cook
gently for 30 minutes till meat is tender. Halve the
aubergines lengthwise and scoop out the centre pulp
leaving a hollow shell, ½-inch thick. Lightly brush
the aubergines with oil and fill the centres with the
meat. Bake in a moderate oven (350° F. Gas
Mark 4) for 25 minutes or till cooked. Serve with
paratha or nan.

KHEEMA GOBI

MINCED LAMB WITH CABBAGE

Preparation time 20 minutes
Cooking time 50 minutes
To serve 4

You will need

1 lb. cabbage
4 onions
1 green chilli
½-inch fresh root ginger
oil for frying
2 cloves
1 cardamom
small stick cinnamom
1 teaspoon chilli powder
2 teaspoons ground coriander seeds
1 teaspoon turmeric powder
1 lb. uncooked lamb, minced
salt to taste
1 tablespoon desiccated coconut
juice of ½ lemon

Shred the cabbage finely, wash and set aside. Finely
mince the onions, green chilli and ginger together
then fry with cloves, cardamom and cinnamon
until lightly brown. Add the chilli powder, coriander and turmeric and cook for five minutes. Add
the meat and salt. Cover with a lid and simmer until
the meat in nearly cooked. Add the cabbage and
coconut. Continue to cook until the cabbage is
ready. Squeeze lemon juice into the pan and mix
well. Serve with roti and chutney.

KOFTA TAMATAR

MEAT BALLS IN TOMATO SAUCE

(Illustrated in colour on page 114)

Preparation time   20 minutes
Cooking time   45 minutes
To serve   4

You will need

small bunch coriander leaves
4 mint leaves
2 green chillis
1 clove garlic
½ teaspoon chilli powder
¼ teaspoon turmeric powder
½ teaspoon salt
½ teaspoon ground ginger
2 slices fresh white bread, grated
1¼ lb. minced beef
flour for coating
1 egg
oil for deep frying

FOR THE SAUCE

1 lb. tomatoes
oil or butter for frying
1 heaped teaspoon flour
5 black peppercorns
1 stick cinnamon
¼ teaspoon chilli powder
salt to taste
4 drops red food colouring (optional)

Finely mince the coriander, mint leaves and chillis, crush the garlic. Put into a mixing bowl with the chilli powder, turmeric, salt, ginger, breadcrumbs and minced beef. Mix well and set aside for at least 20 minutes. Form the mince mixture into small balls. Roll them in flour and dip in the beaten egg. Prepare the gravy by first skinning, chopping and sieving the tomatoes. Heat a little oil or butter in a saucepan, add the flour and cook for a few seconds. Do not allow it to brown. Add the tomatoes, peppercorns, cinnamon, chilli powder and salt. Stir over a gentle heat until well cooked and thick. Add colouring to gravy if desired.
Heat oil and deep fry the balls until cooked and golden. Drain and serve with the gravy poured over.

Potato chops

ALU CHOP

POTATO CHOPS

Preparation time   30 minutes
Cooking time   40 minutes
To serve   4

You will need

2 lb. potatoes
salt to taste
oil for frying
1 large onion
1 clove garlic
½-inch fresh root ginger
½ teaspoon caraway seeds
1 teaspoon ground coriander
½ teaspoon garam masala
½ teaspoon turmeric powder
8 oz. lean beef, minced
1 tomato
salt to taste
1 teaspoon freshly chopped mint
1 egg
breadcrumbs for coating

Boil potatoes. Drain and add salt. Mash until quite smooth. Meanwhile heat oil and fry the chopped onion and crushed garlic till light brown. Add minced ginger and caraway seeds, fry for two minutes and add the coriander, garam masala, turmeric and minced meat. Fry well until meat is quite brown. Add chopped tomato and correct the seasoning.

Simmer till cooked and dry. Mix in chopped mint, leave to cool. Now, using well floured hands divide the mashed potato into eight portions. Form each portion into a ball, flatten in the palm of the hand and place a helping of meat mixture in the centre. Gather the sides together and enclose the meat completely with the potato. Pat into a flat, round or oval shape. Dip in beaten egg and coat with breadcrumbs. Shallow fry in hot oil or fat till pale gold. Serve with chutney and mixed salad.

Stuffed tomatoes

TAMATAR BHARWAN

STUFFED TOMATOES

Preparation time   15 minutes
Cooking time   1¼ hours
To serve   6

You will need

2 onions
1 green chilli
1 clove garlic
butter for frying
½ tablespoon flour
½ teaspoon pepper
1½ teaspoons chilli powder
pinch of salt
1 lb. uncooked lamb, minced
½ teaspoon ground ginger
½ teaspoon ground cinnamon
½ teaspoon ground cloves
6 large tomatoes

Mince onions and green chilli finely, crush garlic. Fry onions and chillis in a little butter till golden. Add flour and fry for a minute or two. Now add pepper, chilli powder, salt, meat, garlic, ginger, cinnamon and cloves. Cook till meat is tender. Meanwhile, slice off the tops of the tomatoes and scoop out pulp. Reserve tomato cases and tops. Add pulp to meat. Dust each tomato case with a little salt and stand upside down for a minute or two. Fill the tomato cases to the top with meat. Cover with tops, arrange in a greased, shallow baking dish and bake in a moderate oven (350° F. — Gas Mark 4) for 20 minutes.

KHEEMA BHINDI BHUJIA

MINCED LAMB WITH OKRA

(Illustrated in colour on page 47)

Preparation time   10 minutes
Cooking time   45 minutes
To serve   4

You will need

1 lb. okra
1 teaspoon turmeric powder
1 lb. uncooked lamb, minced
8 oz. onions
2 green chillis
oil for frying
salt to taste
1 teaspoon cummin seeds

Wash and top and tail okra. Add the turmeric powder and meat to the okra; mix and set aside. Slice onions and finely mince the chillis. Fry the onions in a little oil until slightly brown. Add chillis, salt and meat mixture. Fry until golden brown. Lower the heat and cook until the meat is tender. Roast the cummin seeds, crush and sprinkle over the meat before serving.

DAHI KOFTA

MEAT BALLS IN YOGHURT

Preparation time 10 minutes
Cooking time 15 minutes
To serve 4

You will need

1 onion
2 green chillis
1-inch root ginger
1 clove garlic
2 teaspoons chopped coriander leaves
1¼ lb. lean beef, minced
½ teaspoon ground cummin seeds
1 teaspoon ground coriander seeds
½ teaspoon turmeric powder
¼ teaspoon ground cloves
¼ teaspoon ground cinnamon
1 egg
2 slices white bread, crumbed
salt to taste
oil for frying
4 cartons yoghurt

Mince the onion, chillis, ginger and garlic. Put into a bowl with all the ingredients except the yoghurt. Mix well and shape into walnut-sized balls. Fry in hot oil and when brown drain well. Put yoghurt into a bowl and beat well. Add the meat balls while still hot. Chill and serve cold. If liked add raisins and blanched almonds for extra flavour.

Meat balls in yoghurt

Spiced meat with potatoes

BHUNA GHOST

DRY LAMB CURRY

Preparation time 10 minutes
Cooking time 45 minutes
To serve 4

You will need

1½ lb. leg of lamb, boned
1 onion
3 green chillis
2 cloves garlic
oil for frying
1 teaspoon garam masala
2 teaspoons ground coriander seeds
½ teaspoon chilli powder
1 tablespoon vinegar
salt to taste
1 tablespoon desiccated coconut, soaked in
1 tablespoon hot water

Cut lamb into cubes. Slice onion finely, mince chillis and garlic. Heat some oil in a pan and fry the onion until golden before adding the chillis and garlic. Fry for two minutes, mix the ground spices with the vinegar and salt and add to the onion, stir and fry gently until the spices are well cooked. Now add the meat and continue to fry gently, stirring every now and then to prevent catching. After 20 minutes add the coconut. Mix well and continue cooking until the meat is tender.

JAL FARAZI

SPICED MEAT WITH POTATOES

Preparation time   15 minutes
Cooking time   20 minutes
To serve   4

You will need

1 large onion
1 clove garlic
1-inch piece fresh root ginger
1 lb. cooked meat
8 oz. potatoes, boiled
3 tablespoons oil
½ teaspoon chilli powder
½ teaspoon garam masala
¼ teaspoon turmeric powder
salt to taste

Finely chop onion and garlic; mince ginger; cut meat and potatoes into inch cubes. Fry onions and garlic in oil to brown. Add ginger, chilli powder, garam masala and turmeric, then fry for a few minutes. Add meat, potatoes and salt and heat thoroughly before serving. This dish should be quite dry with no gravy.

KORMA CURRY

YOGHURT CURRY

Preparation time   10 minutes
Cooking time   1-1½ hours
To serve   4

You will need

1½ lb. lamb or beef
1 onion
2 cloves garlic
2-inch fresh root ginger
oil for frying
½ teaspoon freshly ground black pepper
1 teaspoon ground cummin seeds
2 teaspoons chilli powder
2 cartons yoghurt
salt to taste
juice of ½ lemon

Cut meat into cubes. Mince onion, garlic and ginger finely. Heat some oil in a saucepan and fry onions till golden brown. Add garlic and ginger and fry well. Then add pepper, cummin and chilli powder. Fry for five minutes and add meat. Fry the meat well till brown on all sides. Beat the yoghurt well with salt and add to the meat. Stir well and lower the heat and cook slowly till meat is tender. Add the lemon juice 10 minutes before the end of cooking time.

DHALL AUR GHOSHT CURRY

LENTIL AND MEAT CURRY

Preparation time   10 minutes
Cooking time   1-1½ hours
To serve   4

You will need

8 oz. masoor dhal
1 pint (U.S. 2½ cups) salted water
1½ lb. lamb or beef
salt to taste
1 large onion
2 cloves garlic
1-inch fresh root ginger
oil for frying
½ tablespoon ground coriander seeds
1 teaspoon ground cummin seeds
1½ teaspoon chilli powder
1 teaspoon turmeric powder
¼ teaspoon ground cloves
¼ teaspoon ground cinnamon

Wash and soak the dhal for 30 minutes. Boil in salted water until soft. Cut the meat in cubes, season with salt. Mince the onion, garlic and ginger very finely. Heat some oil in a saucepan and fry the onions until golden. Add the garlic and ginger and fry for 1—2 minutes before adding the ground spices. Fry well for about 10 minutes. Sprinkle with water if the mixture becomes too dry. Now add the meat and fry well. Lower the heat, add the dhal, cover, and cook gently until meat is tender.

KOFTA CURRY

MEAT BALL CURRY

Preparation time 20 minutes
Cooking time 1 hour
To serve 4

You will need

1 onion
2 green chillis
1-inch fresh root ginger
1 clove garlic
1 lb. minced beef
1 teaspoon ground coriander seeds
½ teaspoon turmeric powder
1 teaspoon ground cummin seeds
2 teaspoons ground almonds
2 slices white bread, crumbed
1 egg
good squeeze of lemon juice
salt to taste
oil for frying

FOR THE CURRY

1 onion
2 green chillis
1-inch fresh root ginger
1 clove garlic
oil for frying
1 tablespoon ground coriander seeds
1 teaspoon turmeric powder
2 teaspoons ground cummin seeds
½ teaspoon chilli powder
salt to taste
½ pint (U.S. 1¼ cups) water
1 oz. creamed coconut
4 curry or bay leaves

Mince onion, chillis, ginger and garlic very finely and put in a bowl with all the other ingredients for the meat balls. Mix well and shape into small balls the size of a walnut. Heat some oil in a frying pan and fry meat balls till brown. Drain and keep aside. Now make the curry by finely mincing the onion, chillis, ginger and garlic separately. Fry the onion in a little oil till brown. Add the chillis, ginger and garlic, fry for 1—2 minutes and then add the dry spices and salt. Fry for five minutes, sprinkle with water and continue to fry for another five minutes. Add the water, creamed coconut and curry or bay

leaves. Simmer for 20 minutes adding more water if necessary. Add the meat balls and cook for a further 10 minutes.

BRINJAL CUTLETS

AUBERGINE STUFFED WITH MINCED MEAT

Preparation time 15 minutes
Cooking time 1 hour
To serve 4

You will need

4 aubergines
1 onion
2 green chillis
1 clove garlic
1-inch fresh root ginger
1 sprig fresh mint
oil for frying
1 lb. minced beef
1 thick slice white bread, soaked in water
seasoning

FOR THE TOPPING

egg yolk
breadcrumbs

Grilled meat balls

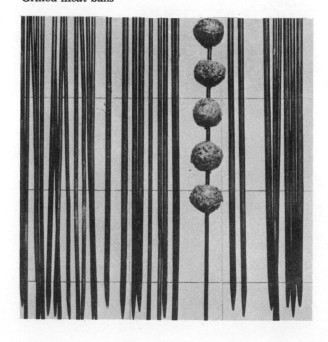

Boil the aubergines in water until nearly cooked (about 15—20 minutes). Drain, cool and cut in half lengthwise. Scoop out pulp and set aside in a bowl. Finely mince the onion, chillis, garlic, ginger and mint leaves. Fry in a little oil for at least five minutes. Add the meat and seasoning then cook till meat is done. Add the meat mixture along with the soaked bread to the aubergine pulp, mix well and stuff into aubergine skins. Brush with beaten egg yolk and top with bread crumbs. Either fry or grill until golden brown.

Stuffed meat balls

KABAB RUKSAND

GRILLED MEAT BALLS

Preparation time   20 minutes
Cooking time   15 minutes
To serve   4

You will need

1 onion
2 green chillis
1 oz. fresh root ginger
1 bunch coriander leaves
1 lb. minced lamb
½ carton yoghurt
½ teaspoon pepper
pinch of ground cloves
¼ teaspoon turmeric powder
2 slices of fresh white bread, grated
salt to taste
melted butter for coating

Mince the onion, green chillis, ginger and coriander leaves finely. Mix them with all the other ingredients in a bowl and leave for two hours. Form mixture into ball-shaped kababs. Brush with melted butter and grill until cooked. Serve hot with slices of lemon.

SHIKAMPOOREE KABAB

STUFFED MEAT BALLS

Preparation time   15 minutes
Cooking time   10-15 minutes
To serve   4

You will need

1 onion
2 cloves garlic
½-inch fresh root ginger
1 teaspoon chilli powder
1 teaspoon turmeric powder
1 teaspoon ground coriander seeds
½ teaspoon ground cummin seeds
½ teaspoon ground almonds
½ teaspoon garam masala
½ teaspoon ground cinnamon
¼ teaspoon ground cardamom
pinch of ground cloves
1 tablespoon gram flour
1 lb. uncooked lamb, finely minced
1 tablespoon dessicated coconut, soaked in
   1 tablespoon hot water
pinch of salt
2 oz. cream cheese
1 tablespoon chopped fresh mint
oil for frying

Chop the onion, garlic and ginger finely. Combine in a mixing bowl with all the other ingredients except the cream cheese, mint and oil. Mix thoroughly to blend.
Blend the cream cheese with the finely chopped mint leaves. Now divide the meat into 12 equal portions. Flatten each portion in the palm of the hand. Put a teaspoon of the cream cheese in the centre and draw up the meat around it. Enclose completely, then flatten gently into a round, flat patty like a hamburger. Fry in a little oil or grill until brown. Serve with onion rings and rice.

MOGHLAI SHAMI KABAB

STUFFED MEAT BALLS

(Illustrated in colour on page 37)

Preparation time   25 minutes
Cooking time   20 minutes
To serve   4

You will need

2 green chillis
2 cloves garlic
2 hard-boiled eggs
1 small onion
1 lb. minced beef
2 large slices white bread, grated
1 teaspoon garan masala
½ teaspoon turmeric powder
½ teaspoon ground ginger
salt to taste
squeeze of lemon juice
1 egg
oil for frying

FOR THE GARNISH

lightly fried onion rings
wedges of raw carrot

Mince the chillis finely; crush the garlic; finely chop the hard-boiled eggs and onion. In a bowl, mix the meat well with the breadcrumbs, garam másala, turmeric, chillis, garlic, ginger, salt, lemon juice and

Skewered meat patties

raw egg. Combine the chopped hard-boiled egg and onion for the filling. Shape the meat into balls and flatten in the palm of the hand. Put a little of the egg and onion mixture into the middle and close on all sides. Flatten and shape to form a patty. Heat some oil in a frying pan and fry the kababs on both sides. Serve with onion rings and wedges of raw carrot.

SEEKH KABABS

SKEWERED MEAT PATTIES

Preparation time   10 minutes
Cooking time   10 minutes
To serve   4

You will need

1 large onion
2 cloves garlic
1-inch fresh root ginger
1 tablespoon chopped coriander leaves
1 lb. lean meat, minced
1 tablespoon gram flour
1 teaspoon poppy seeds
1 tablespoon lemon juice
1 teaspoon chilli powder
½ teaspoon freshly ground black pepper
¼ teaspoon ground cinnamon
¼ teaspoon ground cloves
2 teaspoons ground almonds
pinch of nutmeg
salt to taste
1 egg
oil for grilling

Mince the onion, garlic and ginger very finely. Mix all the ingredients together in a bowl and set aside to marinate for 30 minutes. Grease skewers, shape the meat into long cigar shapes and thread on to the skewers, lengthwise. Turn skewers from time to time whilst grilling and keep brushing meat lightly with oil. Before serving slide the kababs gently off the skewers and serve with onion rings and roti.

Stuffed meat balls

Skewered grilled minced meat

GOL SEEKH KABAB

SKEWERED GRILLED MINCED MEAT

(Illustrated in colour opposite)

Preparation time   10 minutes
Cooking time   15 minutes
To serve   4

You will need

1 green chilli
1 large onion
sprig fresh coriander leaves
1 clove garlic
1 lb. minced lean lamb or beef
1 teaspoon chilli powder
1 teaspoon garam masala
2 teaspoons ground coriander seeds
½ teaspoon ground cummin seeds
2 teaspoons ground almonds
½ teaspoon turmeric powder
1 egg
salt to taste

Finely mince the chilli, onion and coriander leaves; crush garlic. Mix with the meat and add all other ingredients. Mould into long sausage shapes and thread lengthways on to skewers. Cook under the grill. Brush occasionally with oil and cook till done. Serve with plain boiled rice and onion slices.

BOTI KABAB

GRILLED LAMB ON SKEWERS

Preparation time   10 minutes
Cooking time   8 minutes
To serve   4

You will need

1½ lb. leg of lamb, boned
1 carton yoghurt
2 teaspoons ground coriander seeds
1 teaspoon freshly ground black pepper
½ teaspoon turmeric powder
1 teaspoon chilli powder
salt to taste
6 small onions

Cut meat into 1-inch cubes. Mix yoghurt with the spices and salt, in a bowl. Put in the meat, mix well and leave to marinate for at least six hours, or better still overnight. Now cut onions into quarters and separate each layer. Alternate cubes of lamb with pieces of onion on skewers, using 2 skewers for each person. Cook under a hot grill for approximately 8 minutes, 4 minutes on each side. Serve with chappatis.

NARGIS KABAB

EGG AND MINCED LAMB

(Illustrated in colour on page 123)

Preparation time   20 minutes
Cooking time   15 minutes
To serve   4

You will need

12 oz. uncooked lamb, minced
1-inch fresh root ginger
2 cloves garlic
1 green chilli
½ teaspoon ground cummin seeds
½ teaspoon ground coriander seeds
¼ teaspoon turmeric powder
½ teaspoon chilli powder
¼ teaspoon ground cinnamon
¼ teaspoon ground cloves
2 slices white bread, grated
salt to taste
1 egg yolk
6 hard-boiled eggs
oil for frying

Put minced meat into a bowl. Finely mince ginger, garlic and chilli and add to the meat with all the ground spices, breadcrumbs, salt and egg yolk. Mix thoroughly. Shell the hard-boiled eggs. Divide meat into six equal portions. Flatten each portion in the palm of the hand. Put a hard-boiled egg in each centre and carefully work the meat up around the egg until enclosed. Heat some oil in a pan and deep fry till golden brown. Garnish with onion rings and serve with chutney.

GHOST KA SALUN

COCONUT MEAT CURRY

Preparation time   15 minutes
Cooking time   1 hour 10 minutes
To serve   4

You will need

1 large onion, finely chopped
1 garlic clove, crushed
3 green chillis, finely chopped
1-inch fresh root ginger, grated
oil for frying
1 rounded teaspoon turmeric powder
1 rounded teaspoon ground cummin seeds
2 rounded teaspoons ground coriander seeds
2 teaspoons chilli powder
1 teaspoon freshly ground black pepper
1½ lb. lean lamb or beef, cut into cubes
½ pint (U.S. 1¼ cups) water
salt to taste
1 oz. creamed coconut

Fry onion, garlic, chillis and ginger lightly for five minutes in some oil. Add the ground spices and fry well. Add the meat and when thoroughly brown add water. Season with salt and simmer till meat is tender. Add the creamed coconut 20 minutes before the end. Adding more water if necessary.

MASALA CHOPS

SPICED LAMB CHOPS

(Illustrated in colour on page 134)

Preparation time   5 minutes
Cooking time   15 minutes
To serve   4

You will need

2 teaspoons ground coriander seeds
1 teaspoon chilli powder
½ teaspoon ground cummin seeds
1 teaspoon turmeric powder
1 clove garlic, crushed
vinegar to mix
4 lamb chops, trimmed
oil for frying or grilling
salt to taste

Mix all the spices with a little vinegar and salt to make a paste and rub well on both sides of the chops. Leave for 20 minutes. Then fry in a little oil or grill and season with salt. Serve with plain boiled rice, fried onions and salad.

MUTTON PUDDING

Preparation time   15 minutes
Cooking time   1½ hours
To serve   4

You will need

1½ lb. leg of lamb, boned
2 lb. potatoes
8 oz. carrots
¼ pint (U.S. ⅔ cup) water
1 egg
1 teaspoon pepper
2 large onions
3 green chillis
1-inch fresh root ginger
2 cloves garlic
1 bunch coriander leaves
oil for frying
salt to taste
2 tablespoons fine breadcrumbs, toasted

Cut the lamb into pieces. Chop half the potatoes and all the carrots. Cook the lamb, potatoes and carrots in the water until the meat is tender and liquid evaporated. Cool and mince the cooked ingredients. Put in a bowl with the egg and pepper. Finely mince the onions, chillis, ginger, garlic and coriander leaves and fry for at least 10 minutes before adding to the meat. Season with salt, mix well and place in a casserole dish. Cover with toasted breadcrumbs and bake in a moderate oven, (375 F. — Gas Mark 5) for 25—30 minutes. Boil and mash the remaining potatoes, season and serve with the lamb.

MUTTON DO PIAZA

LAMB WITH SPICED ONIONS

Preparation time   20 minutes
Cooking time   1 hour
To serve   4-6

You will need

2 lb. best end of lamb, cut into pieces
1 tablespoon vinegar
1 lb. onions
1 lb. tomatoes
1-inch fresh root ginger
3 green chillis
1 small garlic clove
oil for frying
salt to taste
pinch of chilli powder
¼ teaspoon saffron, soaked in a little milk
1 teaspoon chopped coriander leaves

Sprinkle the lamb with vinegar and leave to marinate for an hour. Thickly slice onions; skin and chop tomatoes; finely mince ginger, chillis and garlic. Heat oil in a large pan and put in the lamb pieces. Sprinkle with salt and chilli powder and fry until well browned. Add onions, ginger, garlic, chillis and saffron. Cover and cook until onions turn golden brown. Add tomatoes and simmer till lamb is tender and the liquid absorbed. Add coriander leaves and cook uncovered for five minutes.

Lamb with chick peas

Soak chick peas in water for 24 hours. Par-boil in 1½ pints of water and drain. Chop onion, crush garlic, mince ginger finely. Cut lamb into cubes and chop tomatoes. Heat oil in a pan and fry the onion for four minutes. Add garlic and ginger and fry for another minute. Add the ground spices, lamb and tomatoes. Cook for 15 minutes. Add water and lemon juice, chick peas and salt. Simmer till gravy is thick and meat tender.

CHANNA MUTTON

LAMB WITH CHICK PEAS

Preparation time   15 minutes
Cooking time   50 minutes
To serve   4

You will need

1 lb. chick peas
1½ pints (U.S. 3¾ cups) water
1 onion
1 clove garlic
1-inch fresh root ginger
1½ lb. leg of lamb, boned
2 ripe tomatoes
oil for frying
1 teaspoon garam masala
½ teaspoon ground cummin seeds
1 teaspoon chilli powder
¾ pint (U.S. 2 cups) water
juice of ½ lemon
salt to taste

MOGHLAI CHOPS

LAMB CHOPS
MOGHUL STYLE

Preparation time   10 minutes
Cooking time   15 minutes
To serve   4

You will need

1 carton yoghurt
1 teaspoon chilli powder
1 teaspoon garam masala
1 clove garlic, crushed
½-inch fresh root ginger, finely chopped
1 teaspoon fresh coriander leaves, finely
  chopped
salt to taste
4 lamb chops
oil for frying

Mix the yoghurt with the spices and salt and use to marinate the lamb chops, for about 30 minutes. Heat some oil in a pan and fry the chops along with marinade until cooked.

BATATA GOSHT

CURRIED MEAT WITH POTATOES

Preparation time   15 minutes
Cooking time   1 hour 10 minutes
To serve   4

You will need

1½ lb. lamb or beef
2 onions
1-inch fresh root ginger
2 garlic cloves
2 tomatoes
4 potatoes
oil for frying
1 teaspoon turmeric powder
1 teaspoon garam masala
2 teaspoons ground coriander seeds
4 cloves
2 cardamoms
1 teaspoon chilli powder
1 cartoon yoghurt
salt to taste

Trim the meat and cut into 1½-inch cubes. Slice the onions; finely mince the ginger and garlic; chop the tomatoes and quarter the potatoes if they are particularly large. Heat some oil in a saucepan and fry the onions until pale golden. Then add the

minced ginger and garlic together with the dry spices. Fry for 10 minutes and add meat and cook till brown and dry. Add tomatoes and yoghurt to the meat and simmer for 20 minutes until the meat is almost cooked. Add the potatoes, season with salt and cook till the potatoes are done.

PALAK GOSHT

CURRIED MEAT WITH SPINACH

(Illustrated in colour on page 143)

Preparation time   15 minutes
Cooking time   1-1¼ hours
To serve   4

You will need

1½ lb. spinach
3-4 tablespoons oil
1 teaspoon sugar
1½ lb. leg of lamb boned and cut into 1-inch pieces
¼ pint (U.S. ⅔ cup) milk
salt to taste
½ teaspoon chilli powder
2 teaspoons ground coriander seeds
1 teaspoon turmeric powder
¼ pint (U.S. ⅔ cup) water
2 teaspoons garam masala

Curried meat with potatoes

Wash spinach and remove coarse stems. Cook without the addition of water, until tender. Drain (reserving the liquid to use later) and sieve to a purée. Heat oil in a saucepan, add a teaspoon of sugar. After a minute or two add the lamb and stir constantly until sealed on all sides. Add the milk, salt, chilli powder and coriander. Cook uncovered until the lamb is well browned and fairly dry. Add the spinach and fry well stirring all the time until all the moisture evaporates. Sprinkle with the turmeric and after a minute add the water, together with the liquid from the spinach. Cook gently until the meat is tender, adding more water if necessary. When all the water has evaporated add the garam masala. Cook for a few minutes before serving with roti.

GOBI GOSHT

CURRIED MEAT WITH CAULIFLOWER

Preparation time 15 minutes
Cooking time 1 hour
To serve 4

You will need

1½ lb. lamb
2 large onions
2 cloves garlic
1-inch fresh root ginger
2 tomatoes
oil for frying
1 teaspoon turmeric powder
1 teaspoon chilli powder
1 teaspoon garam masala
1 teaspoon ground coriander
2 tablespoons yoghurt
salt to taste
1 lb. cauliflower
¼ teaspoon garam masala
fresh coriander leaves, chopped

Cut the meat into 1½-inch pieces. Mince together the onion, garlic and ginger; chop tomatoes. Heat some oil in a large pan and fry the onion, garlic and ginger together with the tomatoes, turmeric, chilli powder, garam masala and ground coriander. Fry till the mixture turns a deep brown and the oil separates. Add the meat and fry for five minutes.

Beat the yoghurt, add to the meat with salt and cook gently for 25 minutes. Cut the cauliflower into sprigs and add to the meat. Simmer for 20 minutes until both cauliflower and meat are tender. Sprinkle with garam masala and chopped coriander leaves before serving. Serve with plain boiled rice.

KHANDANI GOSHT

DRY LAMB CURRY WITH YOGHURT

Preparation time 10 minutes
Cooking time 50 minutes
To serve 4

You will need

1½ lb. lamb
2 green chillis
8 oz. onions
1 large tomato
small bunch of coriander leaves
oil or ghee for frying
½ teaspoon turmeric powder
2 teaspoons ground coriander seeds
pinch ground cloves
1 teaspoon garam masala
pinch ground cardamom seeds
1 teaspoon ground cummin seeds
2 cartons yoghurt
sprig of mint leaves
sprig of curry leaves
pinch of ground cinnamon
salt to taste

Cut the lamb into 1-inch cubes. Finely chop the chillis and onions. Chop the tomato and coriander leaves. Heat some oil or ghee in a heavy pan and fry the chillis. Add the onions and cook gently without browning. Add the lamb and fry for about 10 minutes. Add the tomato and cook until the liquid evaporates. Add the turmeric, coriander, cloves, half the garam masala, cardamoms, cummin, yoghurt, chopped coriander leaves, mint leaves, curry leaves, cinnamon and salt. Cook uncovered at a moderate temperature until the meat is cooked and the yoghurt evaporated.
Sprinkle with remaining garam masala and serve hot with chapattis.

PATHANI-PETHA-GOSHT

MEAT AND PUMPKIN CURRY

Preparation time   30 minutes
Cooking time   1¼ hours
To serve   4

You will need

1½ lb. beef or lamb
1 teaspoon saffron, soaked in
    1 tablespoon water
1 oz. each pistachios, almonds, raisins
2 cloves garlic
1-inch fresh root ginger
2 onions
1½ lb. pumpkin
    or marrow
oil for frying
2 sticks cinnamon
2 cardamoms
1 teaspoon chilli powder
pinch of salt

Trim meat and cut into cubes. Soak saffron in the water for an hour. Finely mince or chop pistachios, almonds, raisins, garlic and ginger. Chop onions; dice pumpkin or marrow and fry onions in a little oil until golden. Add nuts, raisins, garlic and ginger. Continue to fry for a few minutes then add meat,

Meat and pumpkin curry

pumpkin, cinnamon, cardamoms, chilli powder and salt. Cook until pumpkin is completely pulped and meat tender. Add saffron, cook for a further 10 minutes and serve.

BHUNA MUTTON CURRY

FRIED LAMB CURRY

Preparation time   20 minutes
Cooking time   1 hour
To serve   4

You will need

1½ lb. leg of lamb, boned
2 cartons yoghurt
1 teaspoon chilli powder
½ teaspoon turmeric powder
2-inch fresh root ginger
2 cloves garlic
2 onions
salt to taste
½ teaspoon ground cinnamon
¼ teaspoon ground cloves
¼ teaspoon ground cardamoms
¼ teaspoon ground cummin seeds
1 oz. creamed coconut
small bunch coriander leaves
sprig of mint

Cut meat into small cubes. Mix yoghurt, chilli powder and turmeric. Finely mince ginger, garlic and onions. Put lamb, yoghurt mixture, ginger, garlic, half the onion and salt in a pan. Cook gently until lamb is nearly tender. Fry the remaining onion until golden and add the ground spices. Cook for five minutes and add to the lamb and continue cooking until tender. Lastly add chopped coriander and mint leaves, mix well and serve.

PARSEE GOSHT

PARSEE STEW

Preparation time   20 minutes
Cooking time   1 hour
To serve   4

You will need

2 potatoes
2 carrots
oil for frying
8 oz. spring onions, trimmed
1 large onion
2 tomatoes
1½ lb. lamb
4 oz. bacon
4 oz. peas
½ tablespoon flour
¼ pint (U.S. ⅔ cup) stock
salt to taste
½ teaspoon chilli powder

Cut the potatoes and carrots into large pieces and fry with the spring onions for five minutes. Set aside. Slice the onion, chop the tomatoes, dice the bacon and cut the lamb into cubes. Fry the onion for 10 minutes and add the tomatoes, lamb and bacon. Simmer for 10 minutes, add fried potatoes and carrots; spring onions and peas. Cook for a further 10 minutes. Blend the flour with the stock and add to the pan. Season with salt and chilli powder. Stir and cook gently for 25 minutes until meat and vegetables are cooked and the gravy is thick. Serve with roti or nan.

GOSHT CURRY

MEAT CURRY

Preparation time   25 minutes
Cooking time   1¼ hours
To serve   4

You will need

1½ lb. stewing steak
2 tablespoons desiccated coconut, soaked in
    ½ pint (U.S. 1¼ cups) hot milk
2 large onions
2 green chillis
½-inch fresh root ginger
2 cloves garlic
oil for frying
1 teaspoon turmeric powder
2 teaspoons ground cummin seeds
½ teaspoon crushed peppercorns
salt to taste

Parsee stew

Trim the meat into large cubes. Squeeze the coconut out of the milk, reserving only the milk. Mince the onions, chillis, ginger and the garlic. Fry the onions for 10 minutes and then add the green chillis and ginger. Fry for five minutes and add the turmeric, cummin, garlic and peppercorns. Fry well for five minutes and add the meat. Fry the meat until brown on all sides. Pour in the coconut milk and simmer until the meat is cooked. Season with salt and serve hot with chappatis and sliced red pepper.

Meat curry

PORK VENDALU

PICKLED PORK

Preparation time 15 minutes
Cooking time 1½—2 hours
To serve 4

You will need

2 lb. lean pork
2 large garlic cloves
2 rounded teaspoons chilli powder
1 teaspoon turmeric powder
1½ teaspoons dry mustard
1 teaspoon ground cummin seeds
1 pint (U.S. 2½ cups) vinegar
salt to taste

Cut pork into small cubes. Crush the garlic and mix with the spices and vinegar. Put pork into a bowl, cover with the spiced vinegar and leave to soak for 2 hours. Transfer to a saucepan, put on the stove and cook very gently until tender.

MIRCHI FRY

CHILLI FRIED MEAT

Preparation time 10 minutes
Cooking time 30-40 minutes
To serve 4

You will need

1 lb. chuck steak
oil for frying
1 onion, sliced
1 clove garlic, crushed
1-inch fresh root ginger, thinly sliced
2-3 green chillis, slit lengthwise
salt to taste
1 green pepper, sliced
juice of ½-1 lemon

Cut the beef into very thin slices. Heat some oil in a frying pan and fry the onion and garlic for about five minutes, add the ginger and chillis, and fry well before adding the beef. Fry the beef well till brown

on all sides. Add salt and the sliced green pepper. Fry for one minute then add the lemon juice and cook, covered till tender. This is a dry dish and should have little or no gravy. If you feel it is too dry sprinkle a little water into the pan.

DUKAR KA CURRY

PORK CURRY

Preparation time 15 minutes
Cooking time 1¼ hours
To serve 4

You will need

1 large onion, finely chopped
oil for frying
2 cloves garlic, crushed
3 green chillis, chopped
1½-inch fresh root ginger, chopped
4 cloves
4 cardamom seeds
1 small piece cinnamon
1 teaspoon turmeric powder
1 teaspoon ground cummin seeds
1 teaspoon chilli powder
2 teaspoons ground coriander seeds
1½ lb. pork tenderloin, cut into cubes
* 1 oz. tamarind, soaked in
    ¼ pint (U.S. ⅔ cup) hot water
¼ pint (U.S. ⅔ cup) of water
salt to taste
___
* Squeeze the pulp and discard. Strain and use the water.

Fry the onion in some oil until golden brown. Add the garlic, chillis, ginger, cloves, cardamoms and cinnamon and fry well. Now add the ground spices and fry till the raw smell disappears. If too dry sprinkle with water. Add the pork and fry briskly. When well browned add the tamarind and cold water. Season with salt and cook gently until pork is tender.

Minced lamb with okra

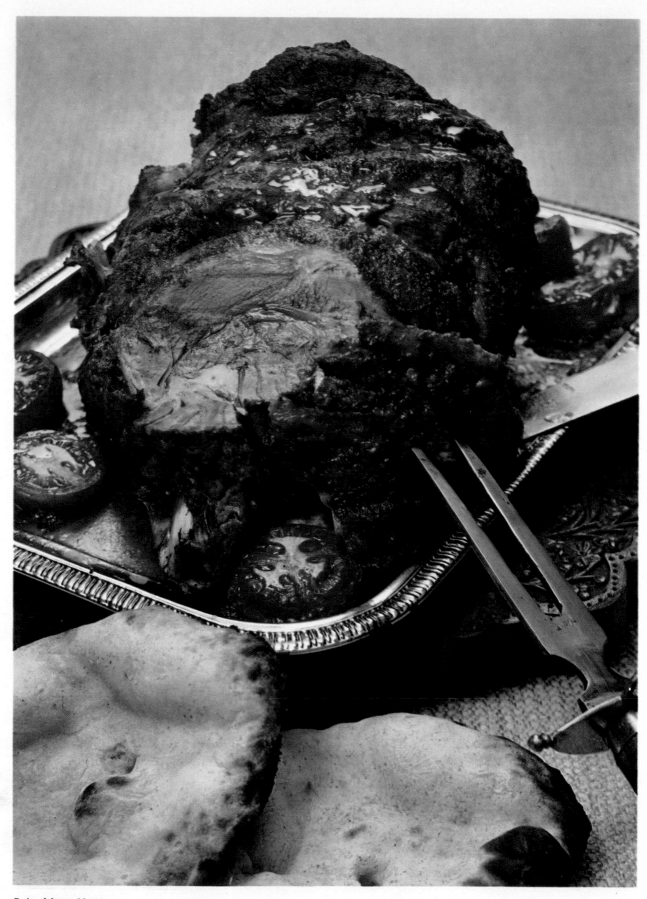

Spiced leg of lamb

MOGHLAI RAAN

SPICED LEG OF LAMB

(Illustrated in colour opposite)

Preparation time　15 minutes
Cooking time　　2-3 hours
To serve　　　　4-6

You will need

4 lb. leg of lamb
4 large onions
4 cloves garlic
2-inch fresh root ginger
1 tablespoon coconut, grated or desiccated
1 tablespoon ground almonds
2 teaspoons ground coriander seeds
2 teaspoons turmeric powder
2 teaspoons garam masala
1 teaspoon ground cummin seeds
2 teaspoons chilli powder
juice of 1 lemon
1 carton yoghurt
2 tablespoons tomato purée
4 cloves
salt to taste
1 tablespoon sultanas

Wash and trim the lamb. With a sharp knife remove the skin and fat. Now mince or grate very finely the onions, garlic and ginger. Put in a bowl and mix in the coconut, almonds, coriander, turmeric, garam masala, cummin seeds, chilli powder, lemon juice, yoghurt and tomato puree. Mix well. Make 5 gashes in the lamb and insert the cloves. Now spread the meat with the mixture and prick all over with a fork. Leave to marinate for at least four hours or overnight. Place meat with marinade in a roasting pan. Sprinkle with salt and sultanas and roast in a moderate oven, (375° F. — Gas Mark 5) for 2—3 hours until meat is very tender or, alternatively, pot roast in a large heavy pan. Baste with marinade occasionally while cooking.

SHAHJEHAN KALEJA

SPICED CHICKEN LIVERS

Preparation time　10 minutes
Cooking time　　40 minutes
To serve　　　　4

You will need

1 lb. chicken livers
8 oz. mushrooms
1 large onion
1 clove garlic

2 tomatoes
butter for frying
$\frac{1}{2}$ teaspoon turmeric powder
$\frac{1}{2}$ teaspoon chilli powder
$\frac{1}{2}$ teaspoon garam masala
1 teaspoon ground coriander seeds
$\frac{1}{2}$ teaspoon ground cummin seeds
2 tablespoons yoghurt
salt to taste

Wash and chop the chicken livers. Wash the mushrooms and slice. Slice the onion finely, crush the garlic and chop the tomatoes. Heat the butter and fry onion and garlic till soft but not brown. Add tomatoes and spices and fry for five minutes then add mushrooms and cook for a further five minutes. Put in the livers, yoghurt and salt. Simmer for 20 minutes. Serve with rice and grilled tomatoes.

Spiced chicken livers

MASALA STEAK

SPICED STEAK

Preparation time   10 minutes
Cooking time   7-10 minutes
To serve   4

You will need

2 cloves garlic
1 onion
2 green chillis
1 tablespoon gound poppy seeds
1 teaspoon garam masala
salt to taste
4 steaks (each weighing 6-8 oz.)

Crush the garlic, finely mince the onion and chillis. Mix garlic, onion, chillis, poppy seed, garam masala and salt. Spread the steaks with this mixture and leave to marinate for an hour. Grill till cooked as desired. Serve with pickled chillis and onion rings.

MADU VINDALU

VINEGAR BEEF CURRY

Preparation time   15 minutes
Cooking time   1½-2 hours
To serve   4

You will need

1 onion
3 cloves garlic
1 tablespoon ground coriander seeds
½ tablespoon turmeric powder
1 teaspoon ground cummin seeds
1 teaspoon ground ginger
2 teaspoons chilli powder
½ teaspoon ground mustard seeds
½ pint (U.S. 1¼ cups) vinegar
1½ lb. stewing steak, cut into cubes
oil for frying
½ pint water

Mince onion and garlic very finely and mix with the ground spices and vinegar. Marinate the beef in this mixture for at least three hours — longer if possible.

Spiced steak

Heat a little oil in a saucepan and add the beef and the marinade with ½ pint (U.S. 1¼ cups) of water. Cover the pan and simmer very gently for 1½-2 hours.

KALEJA TAMATAR

LIVER IN TOMATO SAUCE

Preparation time   10 minutes
Cooking time   40 minutes
To serve   4

You will need

1 lb. liver
1 onion
1 lb. very ripe tomatoes
oil for frying
1 tablespoon vinegar
salt to taste
½ teaspoon chilli powder
½ teaspoon black pepper

Trim and slice the liver thinly. Finely chop the onion; skin and sieve tomatoes. Fry the liver, in a little oil, to brown on both sides. Remove from the pan and set aside. Fry the onion until golden brown. Add the tomatoes, vinegar, salt, chilli powder and pepper. Simmer until the sauce thickens. Add the liver and cook for a further five minutes.

Curried beef and yoghurt

BEEF SUMMA

CURRIED BEEF AND YOGHURT

Preparation time 20 minutes
Cooking time 1½ hours
To serve 4

You will need

1½ lb. beef, cut into slices
1-inch fresh ginger
2 cloves garlic
1 tablespoon ground coriander seeds
1 teaspoon ground poppy seeds
2 teaspoons ground cummin seeds
¼ teaspoon white pepper
2 cartons yoghurt
salt to taste
4 spring onions
oil for frying
1 piece cinnamon
2 cardamom seeds
¼-inch slice creamed coconut
1 tablespoon ground almonds
water to mix
3 red chillis, deseeded
lemon juice

FOR THE GARNISH

onion and pepper, cut into rings

Trim the meat. Mince the ginger, crush the garlic and combine with the ground coriander, poppy, cummin, pepper, yoghurt and salt. Mix with the meat and set aside for five minutes. Finely slice the spring onions and fry in a little oil until slightly brown. Add the cinnamon and cardamoms and fry for one minute before adding the meat. Cook covered for five minutes then remove the lid and cook gently until the meat is nearly done. Mix the coconut and ground almonds with a little water and add to the meat. Simmer for at least another 10 minutes or until the meat is tender. Remove from the heat and add the red chillis and lemon juice to taste. Garnish with rings of onion and green pepper. Serve sauce separately with plain boiled rice or chappatis as an accompaniment.

TALI KALEJA

FRIED SPICED LIVER

Preparation time 5 minutes
Cooking time 20-25 minutes
To serve 4

You will need

1 teaspoon turmeric powder
1 teaspoon chilli powder
½ teaspoon freshly ground black pepper
½-inch fresh root ginger, finely grated
salt to taste
vinegar to mix
1 lb. lambs' liver
oil for frying
1 onion, finely sliced
1 clove garlic, crushed
2 green chillis, slit lengthwise
2 tomatoes, skinned and chopped
salt to taste

Mix the turmeric, chilli powder, black pepper, ginger and salt with a little vinegar to make a paste. Cut the liver into ½-inch thick slices. Wash and dry then rub some of the paste into each slice. Heat a little oil in a frying pan and fry the liver. When cooked remove and set aside. In the same pan fry the onion, garlic and chillis gently, until onions are soft but not brown. Add the tomatoes and salt. Cook for a few minutes until tomatoes are pulped. Add the liver, reheat and serve.

KALEJA MASALA

LIVER CURRY

Preparation time 10 minutes
Cooking time 25 minutes
To serve 4

You will need

1 lb. lamb's liver
1 tablespoon cornflour
2 onions
1 clove garlic
2 tomatoes
oil for frying
½ teaspoon chilli powder
1 teaspoon garam masala
1 teaspoon ground pomegranate seeds
  (optional)
salt to taste

Wash liver and cut into slices. Dry and toss in cornflour. Slice the onions, crush the garlic and chop the tomatoes. Fry the onions until light brown and add the tomatoes, garlic, chilli powder, garam masala and ground pomegranate seeds, if used. Fry for five minutes. Add the liver, season with salt and cook for 20 minutes or till tender.

Curried liver

GURDA KHORMA

CURRIED KIDNEYS

Preparation time 10 minutes
Cooking time 35 minutes
To serve 4

You will need

4 lamb's kidneys
2 onions
2 cloves garlic
3 large tomatoes
oil for frying
1 teaspoon garam masala
1 teaspoon turmeric powder
½ teaspoon chilli powder
½ teaspoon ground cummin seeds
1 teaspoon ground coriander seeds
salt to taste

FOR THE GARNISH

wedges of tomato

Wash, trim and clean the kidneys. Cut into quarters. Slice onions, crush garlic, chop tomatoes. Fry the onion and garlic for five minutes. Add chopped tomatoes, spices and salt and fry for 10 minutes. Put in the kidneys and cook until tender. Garnish with tomato and serve with rice and chappatis or puris.

Curried kidneys

BHEJA CURRY
BRAIN CURRY

(Illustrated in colour on page 144)

Preparation time 15 minutes
Cooking time   1 hour
To serve   4

You will need

3 calves' brains
2 cloves garlic
1-inch fresh root ginger
½ teaspoon chilli powder
½ teaspoon turmeric powder
2 large onions
2 large tomatoes
oil for frying
salt to taste
2 green chillis
small bunch of coriander leaves, chopped
½ teaspoon garam masala
1 teaspoon roasted cummin seeds
½ teaspoon mustard seeds

Soak the brains in cold water for four hours, changing the water frequently. Trim and cut into small pieces. Now crush the garlic, finely mince the ginger and mix with the chilli powder and turmeric. Slice the onions and chop the tomatoes. Heat some oil in a saucepan and fry the onions until golden brown. Sprinkle with a little water, cover and cook until soft. Mash the onions, season with salt and add the tomatoes. Cook, covered, for another five minutes then crush the tomatoes. Add the garlic, ginger, chilli powder, turmeric and garam masala then cook for 10 minutes. Add the pieces of brain carefully turning them over once or twice. Add the whole green chillis, coriander leaves, and a little water if necessary. Simmer on a low heat for 25 minutes. The gravy should be fairly thick. Sprinkle with cummin and mustard seeds. Serve with chappatis or nan and yoghurt.

GURDA MASALA
SPICED KIDNEYS

Preparation time 10 minutes
Cooking time   25-30 minutes
To serve   4

You will need

1 large onion, sliced
oil for frying
2 cloves garlic, crushed
2 green chillis, chopped
1 large green pepper, chopped
8 lamb's kidneys, trimmed, cored and cut into pieces
8 oz. tomatoes, skinned and chopped
salt to taste

Fry the onion in a little oil until golden. Add the garlic and green chillis and fry for a minute or two. Now add the chopped pepper and fry for a few minutes. Add the kidneys and stir before adding the tomatoes and salt. Lower heat, cover and cook gently until tender.

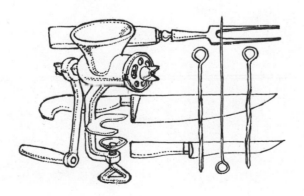

Curried chicken Soup

POULTRY

Poultry is expensive in India and is usually served at parties or on holidays. The best known and most popular dish is 'tandoori' chicken from the North. The method of cooking, can best be described as grilling. This is done in a clay oven called a tandoor. In Western countries the most satisfactory way to cook a tandoori chicken would be to use a rôtisserie or alternatively, it could be roasted in an oven — but with not quite the same results. There are many other excellent chicken dishes from the northern regions of India, many of them cooked with yoghurt or milk. I have also included recipes from the South and West coasts. These recipes are flavoured with coconut milk and vinegar. Chickens are cheap and tender in Britain and they make excellent curries. Though frozen chickens give fairly good results, the best results are obtained by using fresh chickens.

MULLIGATAWNY

CURRIED CHICKEN SOUP

Preparation time   15 minutes
Cooking time   2 hours
To serve   4

You will need

3 lb. chicken
1 clove garlic
1 green chilli
1 onion
1 oz. creamed coconut
salt to taste
1-inch stick cinnamon
2 quarts (U.S. 10 cups) water
3 oz. ground almonds
½ teaspoon garam masala
½ teaspoon black pepper

1 oz. butter
1 tablespoon gram flour
4 oz. cooked rice
chilli powder
1 lemon

Joint the chicken; crush garlic; mince chilli and slice onion. Simmer the chicken pieces in the coconut, salt, cinnamon and water. When the chicken is very tender take it out of the pan, cool, dice and set aside. Return the bones to the pan and cook till liquid is reduced to about 1½ pints (U.S. 3¾ cups). Add garlic, chilli, almonds, garam masala and pepper, stir and bring to the boil. Stain through a sieve and keep aside. Now heat the butter in a saucepan and sauté the onion till lightly brown, add gram flour and blend. Pour in the stock and cook till thickened. Put diced chicken into individual serving bowls. Pour in the soup and serve sprinkled with chilli powder. Serve with boiled rice and lemon wedges.

DHANSAK

CHICKEN WITH LENTILS

(Illustrated in colour opposite)

Preparation time 25 minutes
Cooking time 1¾ hours
To serve 4-6

You will need

1 chicken
6 oz. Tuar dhal
2 oz. each channa, moong and masoor dhal
4 mint leaves
1 pint (U.S. 2½ cups) water
1 aubergine
2 potatoes, peeled
4 onions
4 oz. spinach
4 oz. pumpkin
½ bunch coriander leaves
2-4 green chillis
1-inch fresh root ginger
3 cloves garlic
oil for frying
1 teaspoon ground cummin seeds
2 teaspoons ground coriander seeds
½ teaspoon ground cloves
½ teaspoon ground cinnamon
1 teaspoon turmeric powder
1 teaspoon chilli powder
¼ teaspoon fenugreek
¼ teaspoon mustard seeds
2 bay leaves
salt to taste

Joint the chicken and soak all the dhal. Place in a large, heavy saucepan with mint leaves and water. Chop the aubergine, potatoes, one onion, spinach and pumpkin; add to the chicken, cover and cook very gently. When the chicken is tender remove the pieces and keep aside. Pass the sauce through a sieve adding a little water if it is too thick. While the chicken is cooking, bake one onion in the oven. When tender remove the skin and mince it very finely with the coriander leaves, green chillis, ginger and garlic. Chop the two remaining onions and fry them in a little oil until golden. Add the finely minced ingredients and fry for one or two minutes. Put in the remaining spices and bay leaves and fry for two more minutes. Add the strained dhal, season with salt and simmer gently for 30 minutes. Ten minutes before the end of the cooking time add the chicken pieces.

This is a festive dish among the Parsee community in India and is served with seasoned fried rice, crisply fried meat balls, chutney and a salad made from chopped onions, tomatoes, coriander leaves and green peppers.

MOGHLAI MURGHA

SPICED CHICKEN CURRY

Preparation time 30 minutes
Cooking time 1¼ hours
To serve 4-6

You will need

3 lb. chicken
2-inch fresh root ginger
2 cloves garlic
pinch of salt
½ tablespoon saffron
1 tablespoon cream
3 cartons yoghurt
4 oz. almonds, blanched
2 oz. hazelnuts
3 large onions
1 lb. potatoes, peeled
oil for frying
2 teaspoons chilli powder

Joint the chicken. Mince ginger and garlic very finely then mix with salt and rub on to chicken pieces. Crush saffron in a mortar or with the end of a rolling pin. Mix with cream and yoghurt. Add to the chicken and mix well. Toast almonds and hazel nuts and chop finely. Chop onions finely and quarter potatoes. Heat some oil in a large saucepan and fry onions until golden brown. Add chicken and yoghurt. Cook until liquid evaporates before adding the nuts and chilli powder. Cook and stir adding a little water if necessary. When the chicken is half-cooked add the potatoes. Continue cooking till chicken is tender and gravy thick.

Chicken with lentils

Northern chicken barbecue

TANDOORI MURGHA

NORTHERN CHICKEN BARBECUE

(Illustrated in colour on opposite page)

Preparation time 15 minutes
Cooking time 1¼ hours
To serve 4-6

You will need

3 lb. chicken
½ teaspoon salt
1 medium-sized onion
1-inch fresh root ginger
2 cloves garlic
1 teaspoon ground coriander seeds
1 teaspoon chilli powder
1 teaspoon garam masala
dash of red colouring
1 carton yoghurt
lemon juice
salt to taste
1 tablespoon melted butter
freshly ground pepper

Remove skin from chicken. Either keep whole or cut into four. Prick flesh with a fork and sprinkle with ½ teaspoon salt. Mince or grate the onion, ginger and garlic, as finely as possible. Mix with coriander, chilli powder, garam masala, colouring and salt. Add yoghurt and enough lemon juice to make a fairly thick paste. Make a few gashes on the legs and breast of the bird and rub with the mixture.

Chicken and lentil curry

Leave to marinate for 4—5 hours. Grease a baking tin and cook in a moderate oven (350° F. — Gas Mark 4) allowing 25 minutes per lb. Baste occasionally with the mixture. Half-way through the cooking time brush with butter and sprinkle with freshly ground pepper. Serve on a bed of saffron rice garnished with onion rings and lemon, accompanied by nàn and sliced tomato salad.
The use of a rôtisserie gives better results.

MASOOR KA MURGH

CHICKEN AND LENTIL CURRY

Preparation time 20 minutes
Cooking time 1½ hours
To serve 4-6

You will need

1 chicken
1 lb. black dhal
3 cloves garlic
4 onions
3 green chillis
4 tomatoes
oil for frying
1 teaspoon ground cummin seeds
1 teaspoon ground coriander seeds
½ teaspoon chilli powder
1 teaspoon garam masala
juice of 1 lemon
1 teaspoon turmeric powder
1 teaspoon chopped coriander leaves
1 pint (U.S. 2½ cups) plus 2 tablespoons water
salt to taste

Joint the chicken. Wash and soak the dhal in water for an hour before use. Mince the garlic and onions. Chop the chillis and tomatoes. Fry the onions and garlic in a little oil until golden brown. Add the cummin seeds, coriander, chilli, garam masala, lemon juice and turmeric. Fry well and add 2 tablespoons water and cook until dry. Put in the chicken and fry for 10 minutes. Drain dhal and add. Mix well then add the coriander leaves, chillis, tomatoes and salt to taste. Pour in a pint of hot water and simmer covered until the chicken is tender. Add a little more water if necessary. Serve with rice.

CHICKEN PIDEE

CHICKEN CURRY
WITH DUMPLINGS

Preparation time 15 minutes
Cooking time 1 hour
To serve 4

You will need

1 medium-sized chicken
2 large onions
oil for frying
2 teaspoons chilli powder
1 teaspoon black pepper
½ teaspoon ground cinnamon
½ teaspoon ground cloves
1 teaspoon turmeric powder
1 oz. creamed coconut
1 pint (U.S. 2½ cups) water
salt to taste
Chopped coriander leaves

FOR THE DUMPLINGS

4 oz. rice flour
water to mix
pinch of salt
2 oz. rice

Joint the chicken. Slice the onions finely and fry in a little oil until golden brown. Add all the dry spices and fry for five minutes. Add the chicken and fry

for 2—3 minutes then add the creamed coconut, water and salt. Bring to the boil and then simmer very gently until chicken is cooked.

Meanwhile mix the rice flour with enough water to make a stiff paste, season with salt and shape into small dumplings. Place carefully in the curry 20 minutes before the end of cooking time. Garnish with freshly chopped coriander leaves.

PALAK MURG

SPICED CHICKEN
WITH SPINACH

Preparation time 20 minutes
Cooking time 45 minutes
To serve 4

You will need

1 chicken
2 cloves garlic
2 onions
2 tomatoes
1½ lb. spinach
oil for frying
2 cloves
1 teaspoon ground coriander
dash of pepper
salt to taste
4 tablespoons milk

Chicken curry with dumplings

Spiced chicken with spinach

60

Cut the chicken into joints. Crush garlic, finely mince onions, chop tomatoes, wash and chop spinach. Heat oil and fry onions gently for 10 minutes before adding the spinach, tomatoes, garlic, cloves, coriander, pepper and salt. Cook for five minutes and add milk. Arrange chicken pieces on the spinach. Cover tightly and cook on a low heat until the chicken is tender. Serve with plain boiled rice.

MURGHI PULAO

CHICKEN PULAO

(Illustrated in colour on page 86)

Preparation time   20 minutes
Cooking time   1¾-2 hours
To serve   4-6

You will need

8 oz. rice
yellow colouring
1 chicken
¾ pint (U.S. 2 cups) chicken stock
1 teaspoon chilli powder
½ teaspoon ground cinnamon
1 teaspoon black pepper, crushed
½ teaspoon ground cummin seeds
½ teaspoon ground cloves
1 carton yoghurt
salt to taste
oil for frying
½ teaspoon saffron, soaked in
   a little lemon juice
2 oz. raisins
2 oz. almonds
8 oz. onions, sliced
4 oz. potatoes
1 teaspoon garam masala
seasoning

FOR THE GARNISH

4 oz. cooked peas

Wash rice and soak for 30 minutes and then parboil. Add yellow colouring to half the rice and keep aside. Simmer the chicken gently in the stock until tender. Remove the chicken from the pan, save the liquid, joint the chicken. Now mix the next five ingredients with the yoghurt and salt. Coat the chicken pieces with the mixture. Put a little oil in a frying pan and fry the chicken gently. Add half the saffron, remove the mixture from the pan and set aside. Fry raisins and almonds. Fry onions and potatoes.
Put layers of yellow-coloured rice, half the onions, potatoes and white rice, each sprinkled with a little garam masala, into an oven-proof dish. Top with the chicken joints. Cover with ½ pint (U.S. 1¼ cups) of the reserved chicken stock, season and cover with lid or foil. Cook in a moderate oven (350° F. — Gas Mark 4) till rice is cooked and all liquid absorbed. Transfer to a serving dish and add the peas.

DAHI MURGH

CHICKEN WITH YOGHURT

Preparation time   15 minutes
Cooking time   30 minutes
To serve   4-6

You will need

1 medium-sized chicken
3 cartons yoghurt
salt to taste
8 oz. onion
1-inch fresh root ginger
3 garlic cloves
2 green chillis
oil for frying
½-inch slice creamed coconut
1 tablespoon poppy seeds
juice of 1 lemon

Joint the chicken. Place in a pan with the yoghurt and salt and cook gently until tender. Meanwhile, finely mince the onion, ginger, garlic and chillis. Fry the onion gently for 10 minutes. Add the ginger, garlic, chillis, coconut and poppy seeds and fry for a further 10 minutes. Add the chicken and continue to cook over a moderate heat for 10 minutes. Mix in the lemon juice. Serve with nan or chappatis.

Spiced chicken kebabs

South coast chicken curry

MURGH TIKKA

SPICED CHICKEN KABABS

Preparation time 10 minutes
Cooking time 8-10 minutes
To serve 6

You will need

1 large chicken
2 onions
2 cloves garlic
1-inch fresh root ginger
1 carton yoghurt
1 teaspoon chilli powder
1 teaspoon garam masala
1 teaspoon ground coriander seeds
few drops red colouring
juice of 1 lemon
salt to taste

FOR THE GARNISH

lemon wedges
lettuce leaves
sliced tomato and onion

Remove skin from chicken and, with a sharp knife, remove meat from the bones. Cut into suitable-sized pieces for serving. Grate or mince the onions, garlic and ginger as finely as possible. Mix with the yoghurt, chilli, garam masala and coriander. Add the colouring and season with salt and lemon juice. Coat the chicken with this mixture and leave to

marinate overnight. Thread chicken pieces on skewers and cook over a barbecue or under a grill for 8—10 minutes till tender. Garnish with lemon wedges, lettuce and tomato and onion slices. Serve with chappatis.

MADRAS MURGH

SOUTH COAST CHICKEN CURRY

Preparation time 15 minutes
Cooking time 1¼ hours
To serve 4-6

You will need

1 medium-sized chicken
2 onions
1½-inch fresh root ginger
2 cloves garlic
2 potatoes, peeled
oil for frying
½ teaspoon turmeric powder
2 tablespoons ground cummin seeds
1 teaspoon garam masala
2 green chillis
a sprig of curry leaves
  or 2 bay leaves
1 pint (U.S. 2½ cups) water
4 oz. creamed coconut
salt to taste

Joint the chicken. Finely mince onions, ginger and garlic separately. Dice potatoes. Fry onions and ginger in oil until lightly browned. Add garlic, turmeric, cummin and garam masala. Fry for three minutes. Slit green chillis and add together with the curry leaves. Now add chicken pieces and fry till well browned. Pour in the water and cook till half done. Add potatoes and continue to simmer. Add the creamed coconut 15 minutes before the end of cooking time. Add salt to taste and serve with rice and chutney.

DUM MURGI

STUFFED WHOLE CHICKEN

Preparation time   25 minutes
Cooking time   1¼ hours
To serve   4

You will need

¼ teaspoon saffron
½ teaspoon ground nutmeg
¼ teaspoon ground cardamom seeds
1 tablespoon milk
1 medium-sized chicken
scant ½ pint (U.S. 1¼ cups) water

FOR THE STUFFING

3 large onions
2 oz. almonds
2 green chillis
1-inch fresh root ginger
3 hard-boiled eggs
2 oz. raisins
oil for frying
4 oz. cooked peas
salt to taste

FOR THE MASALA

2 large onions
2 cloves garlic
oil for frying
½ teaspoon ground cloves
1 teaspoon black pepper
1 teaspoon chilli powder
½ teaspoon ground cinnamon
¼ teaspoon ground cardamom seeds
¼ teaspoon ground coriander seeds
½ teaspoon turmeric powder
1 tablespoon yoghurt

Mix the saffron, nutmeg and cardamom with the milk and spread inside the chicken. To prepare the stuffing peel and chop the onions, blanch and skin the almonds, mince the chillis and the fresh root ginger, then shell and chop the hard-boiled eggs. Wash, stone and chop the raisins. Heat a little oil and fry the onions until slightly brown, add the almonds, chillis, ginger, raisins, peas and salt. Mix well and add the eggs, then stuff the chicken with this mixture. Sew up the open ends with clean white cotton. Heat oil in a large heavy saucepan and fry the chicken on all sides until brown; remove it on to a plate, and cook the masala in the same pan. To prepare the masala mince or very finely chop the onions with the garlic and fry in a very little oil for a few minutes. Stir in all the dry ingredients and continue cooking for 5 minutes. Add the yoghurt, keep stirring and cook for a further 10 minutes. Place the chicken on top of the masala in the pan; add the water, cover with a lid and simmer until the chicken is tender. Garnish with chopped coriander leaves and desiccated coconut.

Stuffed whole chicken

PAHARI MURGH

CHICKEN WITH MINCED MEAT STUFFING

Preparation time   35 minutes
Cooking time   2 hours
To serve   4-6

You will need

1 medium-sized chicken
2-inch fresh root ginger
2 cloves garlic
2 green chillis
1 teaspoon ground coriander
juice of 1 lemon
salt to taste

FOR THE STUFFING

2 tablespoons oil
1 large onion, sliced
1 lb. minced veal or beef
1 carton yoghurt
1 clove garlic *and*
   1-inch piece of root ginger
sprig of mint leaves
½ teaspoon ground coriander
2 green chillis, finely chopped
½ teaspoon ground cardamom seeds
½ teaspoon pepper
¼ teaspoon ground cinnamon
salt to taste
2 pieces cinnamon

FOR THE GARNISH

cashew nuts
hard-boiled eggs

Wash the chicken thoroughly. Finely mince the ginger, garlic and green chillis and mix together with the ground coriander, lemon juice and salt. Rub this mixture on the chicken inside and out, leave for 30 minutes. Prepare the stuffing by heating one tablespoon of the oil in a saucepan; fry the onions until light brown. Add the minced meat and fry for a few minutes. Add all the ingredients except the cinnamon pieces and remaining oil. Cook until the meat is tender. Stuff the chicken with half the mince. Now heat the remaining oil in an iron casserole, add the two pieces of cinnamon and as soon as the oil starts spitting remove from the heat. Cook the chicken in a pan on top of the stove until tender. Put half the remaining mince in the casserole, place the chicken on top of it and put the rest of the mince on top of the chicken. Cover casserole with lid and cook over a low heat until the mince at the bottom turns brown. Remove the lid and place in a hot oven (400 deg F. — Gas Mark 6) to brown the top. Sprinkle with cashew nuts and serve with quartered hard-boiled eggs.

MALAI MURGH

CHICKEN COOKED IN MILK

Preparation time   20 minutes
Cooking time   1 hour 35 minutes
To serve   6-8

You will need

1½ lb. onions
butter for frying
2 oz. almonds, blanched
2 oz. raisins
1 large chicken
2 pints (U.S. 5 cups) milk
1 oz. sugar
salt to taste
1 teaspoon chilli powder
5 egg yolks
¼ pint cream

Slice onions finely. Heat some butter in a large saucepan and fry almonds and raisins gently. Transfer from the pan, fry onions in the same butter until tender but not brown. Set aside. Wipe the chicken well and place in a heavy pan with the milk, simmer until cooked. Take chicken out, allow to cool and remove flesh from carcass. Set aside. Now add sugar, salt and chilli powder to the milk and cook rapidly until liquid is reduced to 1 pint (U.S. 2½ cups). Remove from heat and allow to cool slightly. Beat egg yolks with cream and add to milk, with pieces of chicken, mix gently but well. Check seasoning. Take a large baking dish and spread half the chicken mixture in the bottom. Sprinkle with half the almonds, raisins and onions. Top with another layer of chicken covered with almonds, raisins and onions. Cover with foil and bake in a moderate oven (350° F. — Gas Mark 4) for 30 minutes or until set.

Spiced chicken with yoghurt

MURGH KHORMA

SPICED CHICKEN
WITH YOGHURT

Preparation time   15 minutes
Cooking time   1 hour
To serve   4-6

You will need

1 medium-sized chicken
2 large onions
2 cloves garlic
1-inch fresh root ginger
1 lb. tomatoes
2 dry red chillis
6 cloves
2 sticks cinnamon
2 cardamoms
oil for frying
8 peppercorns
2 cartons yoghurt
1 teaspoon turmeric powder
pinch of saffron
salt to taste

FOR THE GARNISH

1 tablespoon blanched almonds

Skin and joint the chicken. Slice the onions, garlic and ginger finely. Chop the tomatoes. Cut the chillis into ¼-inch pieces. Fry the cloves, cinnamon and cardamons in a little oil. Add the onions and fry until golden brown. Add peppercorns, garlic, ginger and chillis and fry for five minutes. Add chicken pieces and fry until brown. Put yoghurt in a bowl, add turmeric and saffron and beat until smooth. Add to the chicken together with the tomatoes and salt. Cover saucepan tightly and cook on a low heat until the chicken is tender. Uncover and cook for 10 minutes. Garnish with almonds. Serve with tandoori rotis.

KAJU MURGH

CHICKEN
WITH CASHEWNUTS

Preparation time   15 minutes
Cooking time   1 hour 10 minutes
To serve   4

You will need

1 medium-sized chicken
½ pint (U.S. 1¼ cups) stock or water
½ bunch coriander leaves
2 green chillis
2 cloves garlic
1-inch fresh root ginger
oil for frying
2 large onions, minced
½ teaspoon garam masala
¼ teaspoon ground cummin seeds
2 cartons yoghurt
2 whole cardamoms
6 oz. ground cashewnuts
salt to taste

Joint the chicken, and simmer till tender in stock. Strain and reserve a teacup of the stock. Mince together finely, the coriander leaves, green chillis, garlic and ginger. Heat oil in a heavy pan and fry the onions, minced spices, garam masala and ground cummin, till golden. Beat the yoghurt and combine with the reserved stock, add to the pan and bring to the boil. Put in the chicken and cardamoms and simmer for a few minutes. Add cashew nuts and cook, stirring, till simmering point. Season with salt.

BATAK VINDALOO

DUCK CURRY (1)

Preparation time 10 minutes
Cooking time 1 hour
To serve 4

You will need

1 duck
4 small onions
2 medium-sized onions
3 dry red chillis
½-inch fresh root ginger
2 cloves garlic
1 green chilli
oil for frying
1 teaspoon turmeric powder
½ tablespoon ground coriander seeds
½ pint (U.S. 1¼ cups) water
2 tablespoons vinegar
salt to taste
1 oz. creamed coconut

FOR THE GARNISH

lemon butterflies
raw onion slices

Wipe and dry the duck. Slice small onions and quarter the larger ones. Slit red chillis and remove the seeds; finely mince ginger and garlic and slit

Duck curry (1)

the green chilli lengthwise. Heat a little oil in a large saucepan. Fry the sliced onions and red chillis. When the onions are brown add the ginger, garlic, turmeric and coriander. Continue to fry for a few minutes. Mix in the water; add the duck, green chilli, quartered onions and vinegar. Cover and cook gently until nearly done. Remove the lid and cook more rapidly until the gravy thickens. Add salt and coconut. Simmer for a further 10 minutes. Serve with rice and peas. Garnish with lemon butterflies and onion slices. Hand gravy separately.

BATAK PATIA

DUCK CURRY (2)

Preparation time 15 minutes
Cooking time 1 hour 10 minutes
To serve 4

You will need

2-inch fresh root ginger
2 cloves garlic
2 onions
2 green chillis
2 teaspoons ground coriander seeds
1 teaspoon ground cummin seeds
½ teaspoon mustard seeds
2 teaspoons poppy seeds
1 teaspoon chilli powder
½ teaspoon ground cloves
½ teaspoon ground cinnamon
½ teaspoon ground cardamoms
1 teaspoon turmeric powder
water to mix
1 duck
oil for frying
1 tablespoon vinegar
salt to taste

Slice ginger, garlic, onions and chillis finely. Mix all the other spices together with a little water to make a paste. Joint the duck and fry in a little oil until golden brown. Remove from heat and set aside. Fry the onion, ginger, garlic and chillis in a large saucepan until light brown. Add the duck and spice paste then cook for 15 minutes, stirring all the time. Add vinegar, salt, and if required, a little water. Cover and simmer till duck is cooked and gravy thick.

GOA MOLI

GOAN VINEGAR CURRY

Preparation time   15 minutes
Cooking time   1 hour
To serve   4

You will need

1 duck or chicken, cut into pieces
oil for frying
6 medium-sized onions
2-inch fresh root ginger
3 green chillis
3 cloves garlic

FOR THE MASALA

1 teaspoon chilli powder
2 tablespoons ground coriander seeds
2 teaspoons ground cummin seeds
1 teaspoon ground cloves
½ teaspoon ground cardamoms
½ teaspoon ground cinnamom
1 teaspoon turmeric powder
¾ pint (U.S. 2 cups) vinegar
salt to taste

Fry duck or chicken pieces in a little oil until golden brown. Keep aside. Slice onions, ginger and green chillis, crush the garlic and fry for five minutes. Combine the ingredients for the masala with enough vinegar to make a paste, add to the ingredients in the pan and fry for a further 10 minutes. Add the duck and mix well. Add the remaining vinegar and the salt and cook on a low heat till tender.

SHAHI MURGH

CHICKEN COOKED IN YOGHURT

Preparation time   30 minutes
Cooking time   50 minutes
To serve   4-6

You will need

1 medium-sized chicken
2 cloves garlic
1½-inch fresh root ginger
2 green chillis
3 onions
¼ teaspoon saffron
1 dessertspoon milk
oil or ghee for frying
salt to taste
4 tablespoons desiccated coconut, soaked in
    4 tablespoons hot water
3 cartons yoghurt
1 teaspoon chopped coriander leaves
4 cardamoms

Joint the chicken, crush garlic; finely mince ginger and chop green chillis and the onions. Soak saffron in milk.
Fry the chicken pieces in oil or ghee for a few minutes. Add ginger, garlic and salt. Cook very gently until tender for about 30 minutes. Add onions, chillis and strained coconut milk; cover and cook for 10 minutes. Add well-beaten yoghurt, saffron, coriander and cardamoms and simmer for 10 more minutes. If the sauce becomes too thin, remove the chicken joints and reduce by rapid boiling.

Spiced herrings

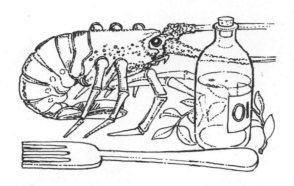

FISH

As almost half of India is a peninsula with a coastline of 2,500 miles it is natural for Indians, especially those living near the sea, to have a partiality for fish. Among sea fish are pomfret, prized for their delicate flavour and firm white flesh; sea salmon, herrings, mullet, mackerel and sardines. Shell fish, especially prawns and crayfish, are plentiful and popular. A small species of shark is a delicacy in southern India but this is an acquired taste.

The people of Bengal are known to be particularly fond of fish. Their state is criss-crossed with rivers and boasts the delta of the Ganges. Bengalis eat both river and sea fish; they use mustard oil for cooking, to give their food a unique flavour. Goan fish curry, hot and pungent, and the Malabar coast fish and prawn curry, rich with coconut milk, are equally appetising. The Zoroastrians (Parsees) around Bombay are famous for their fillets of pomfret, covered with coriander and coconut chutney, wrapped in banana leaves and then steamed. The banana leaf lends a delicate fragrance to the fish, but now-a-days foil is often used with a consequent loss of taste — but added convenience. Bombay duck is not a bird but a small fish made into a tasty curry and when sun-dried, is eaten as an accompaniment to a curry.

In England both cod and haddock make good curry. Plaice tends to break up during cooking but good fresh sole is excellent, being nearest equivalent to pomfret. Canned prawns are good but must be added to the curry at the last minute to prevent over-cooking.

MASALA BANGRA

SPICED HERRINGS

Preparation time   5 minutes
Cooking time   10 minutes
To serve   2

You will need

2 large herrings
salt
1 onion
1 clove garlic
½ teaspoon turmeric powder
½ teaspoon garam masala
½ teaspoon chilli powder
juice of ½ lemon
oil for frying
chopped coriander leaves

Clean and gut the herrings and sprinkle with salt, keep aside. Grate onion and crush garlic and mix with the turmeric, garam masala and chilli powder. Add the lemon juice to make a paste and spread the fish with this mixture inside and outside. Heat some oil in a frying pan and fry the fish on both sides till golden brown. Sprinkle with chopped coriander leaves.

TALI MACHEE

SPICED FRIED FISH

Preparation time 5 minutes
Cooking time   10 minutes
To serve   4

You will need

4 fish steaks or fillets (use any firm-fleshed type)
4 teaspoons turmeric powder
2 teaspoons chilli powder
salt to taste
vinegar
oil for frying

Wash and dry the fish. Mix turmeric, chilli powder and salt with a little vinegar to make a paste. Rub the paste into both sides of the fish. Heat a little oil in a frying pan and fry the fish until cooked.

TANDOORI MACHI

BAKED SPICED FISH

Preparation time 3 minutes
Cooking time   30 minutes
To serve   4

You will need

2 lb. fillets of cod or haddock
salt to taste
juice of half a lemon
1 carton yoghurt
1 tablespoons vinegar
1 teaspoon garam masala
2 cloves garlic, crushed
1 teaspoon ground cummin seeds
½ teaspoon chilli powder

Wash and dry the fillets. Sprinkle with salt and lemon juice. Set aside for a few minutes to marinate. Combine the yoghurt with the rest of the ingredients. Place the fish in a shallow baking dish. Make two deep gashes across the fillets. Pour the yoghurt mixture over the fish and leave to soak for several hours. Bake in a moderate oven (375° F. — Gas Mark 5) for 30 minutes.

Spiced fish patties

MACHI KABABS

SPICED FISH PATTIES

Preparation time 15 minutes
Cooking time   30 minutes
To serve   4

You will need

1¼ lb. haddock or cod, cooked
1 large onion
2 green chillis
few coriander leaves
2 potatoes, cooked
¼ teaspoon ground ginger
½ teaspoon black pepper
2 eggs
salt to taste
breadcrumbs
fat for frying

Remove bones from the fish and mash finely. Mince the onion, chillis and coriander leaves. Mash the potatoes. Mix the fish, onion, chillis, coriander leaves, potatoes, ginger, pepper, 1 egg and salt. Divide the mixture into 8 portions, roll into balls and flatten into rounds ½-inch thick. Dip in beaten egg and roll in breadcrumbs. Fry in shallow fat till nicely brown on both sides.

DUM MACHEE

SPICED BAKED FISH

Preparation time   10 minutes
Cooking time   1 hour
To serve   4

You will need

1 bream (approximately 2 lb.)
2-inch fresh root ginger
3 green chillis
2 cloves
2 cardamom seeds
12 almonds
1 carton yoghurt
1 teaspoon sugar
salt to taste

Get the fishmonger to clean the fish. Skin and remove the head and tail. Wash and dry the fish and place in a flat casserole dish. Mince the ginger and chillis very finely. Crush the cloves and cardamons coarsely. Blanch, roast and slice almonds. Put yoghurt in a bowl, beat well and add all the spices, almonds, sugar and salt. Mix and pour over the fish. Bake covered in a moderate oven (350° F. — Gas Mark 4) for about 1 hour.

BHUNA MACHEE

FISH FRIED WITH SPICES

Preparation time   15 minutes
Cooking time   30 minutes
To serve   4

You will need

1½ lb. thick fillets of haddock *or*
   other firm white fish
2 large potatoes
2 onions
3 green chillis
1½ teaspoons turmeric powder
salt to taste
oil for frying
1 teaspoon chilli powder
½ pint (U.S. 1¼ cups) water

Cut the fish into cubes. Dice the potatoes, slice onions finely, and slit chillis. Rub the fish with ½ teaspoon turmeric and salt. Heat the oil in a frying pan and cook the fish until golden brown. Drain and set aside. Now heat a little more oil and fry the onions till golden. Add the remaining turmeric and the chilli powder, fry for three minutes. Add the potatoes and salt to taste. Fry for a minute or two before adding the water. When the potatoes are half–cooked add the chillis and fish. Cover and simmer until potatoes are cooked and the gravy thick.

MEEN MOLEE

FISH CURRY WITH COCONUT

Preparation time   20 minutes
Cooking time   25—30 minutes
To serve   4

You will need

oil for frying
1 onion, finely chopped
1 clove garlic, crushed
1-inch fresh root ginger, finely sliced
4 cardamom seeds
6 cloves
1-inch piece of cinnamon
1 level teaspoon turmeric powder
6 green chillis, slit lengthwise
* thick coconut milk from 1 coconut
   (see page 7) *or*
   3 oz. creamed coconut
salt to taste
4 thick cod or haddock steaks
────
* Real coconut milk will give the best results.

Heat some oil in a big frying pan and fry the onion, garlic and ginger lightly, without browning. Add the cardamoms, cloves and cinnamon. After one minute add the turmeric and green chillis. Stir and cook gently for about three minutes. Now add the coconut milk and salt and bring to the boil. Place the fish carefully in the pan and simmer until cooked. Be careful not to break up the fish. The gravy must be thick.

MACHEE KOFTA CURRY

FISH BALL CURRY

Preparation time   15 minutes
Cooking time   45 minutes
To serve   4

You will need

FOR THE FISH BALLS

1 lb. fillet of haddock, steamed
1 potato
1 onion
1-inch fresh root ginger
2 green chillis
1 slice white bread, grated
1 egg, lightly whisked
salt to taste
oil for frying

FOR THE CURRY

1 onion
1-inch fresh root ginger
2 green chillis
oil for frying
2 cloves
1 cardamom
1-inch piece cinnamon
1 teaspoon turmeric powder
2 teaspoons ground coriander
½ teaspoon chilli powder
2 curry leaves
1 teaspoon sugar
juice of ½ lemon
salt to taste
2 oz. creamed coconut
¾ pint (U.S. 2 cups) water

Remove bones and skin from the fish, then flake. Boil the potato, mash and add to the fish. Finely mince the onion, ginger and chillis and add to the fish along with the breadcrumbs, egg and salt. Mix well and mould into walnut-sized balls. Fry the fish balls in oil till golden brown. Drain and set aside. Now make the curry. Slice the onion, mince ginger and chillis finely. Heat some oil in a saucepan and fry the cloves, cardamon and cinnamon for two minutes. Add the onion and fry till golden. Add the ginger and chillis, fry for a further two minutes and add the rest of the spices. Fry well for seven minutes then add sugar, lemon juice, salt, coconut and

Spiced fish bake

water. Bring to the boil and simmer very gently for 30 minutes. Add the fish balls, cook for 10 minutes and serve. Serve with plain boiled rice.

PATRA NI MACHI

SPICED FISH BAKE

Preparation time   20 minutes
Cooking time   20-25 minutes
To serve   4

You will need

2 cloves garlic
3 green chillis
large bunch of coriander leaves
2 oz. creamed coconut
2 teaspoons ground cummin seeds
1 teaspoon sugar
salt to taste
juice of 2 lemons
4 cod steaks

Finely mince the garlic, chillis and coriander leaves, then mix with the coconut, cummin, sugar, salt and lemon juice to make a paste. Clean and wash the fish, rub with salt and set aside for 10 minutes. Now coat the fish on both sides with the paste, put in a baking dish, cover with foil and bake in a moderately hot oven (375° F. — Gas Mark 5) for 20—25 minutes. Serve with sliced tomatoes.

MACHI BAFFATTE

FISH WITH SPICES AND VINEGAR

Preparation time   15 minutes
Cooking time   30 minutes
To serve   4

You will need

2 lb. haddock or cod steaks
2 onions
2 green chillis
1½-inch fresh root ginger
2 cloves garlic
oil for frying
3 tablespoons vinegar
1 stick cinnamon
2 cardamons
¼ teaspoon ground black pepper
salt to taste

FOR THE GARNISH

1 tablespoon chopped coriander leaves

Wash the fish steaks; slice the onions into rings, finely mince the chillis, ginger and garlic. Heat a little oil and fry the onions until golden. Add the chillis, ginger and garlic and fry for five minutes.

Fish in Parsee sauce

Add the vinegar and remaining ingredients and simmer gently for five minutes. Add the fish and, if necessary, 1—2 tablespoons of water. Simmer until fish is cooked and the gravy is thick. Garnish with coriander leaves and serve with rice or bread.

PARSI MACHI

FISH IN PARSI SAUCE

Preparation time   10 minutes
Cooking time   45 minutes
To serve   4

You will need

2 onions
2 cloves garlic
2 green chillis
oil for frying
1 teaspoon ground cummin seeds
¼ pint (U.S. ⅔ cup) water
1 tablespoon rice flour, mixed with
  2 tablespoons water
four 8 oz. cod steaks
salt to taste
3 tablespoons vinegar
2 eggs
2 teaspoons sugar

FOR THE GARNISH

chopped coriander leaves

Slice onions, finely mince garlic and chillis. Heat a little oil in a saucepan, add the onions and fry till brown. Add the garlic, chillis and cummin; cook for five minutes. Pour water into the pan, bring to the boil and simmer for 10 minutes. Add the rice flour-paste and continue to cook until the gravy thickens. Add the fish and salt; cook till tender. Remove the pan from the heat. Beat the vinegar, eggs and sugar together and pour over fish. Re-heat without boiling. Garnish with chopped coriander leaves.

JINGA SALAD

CURRIED PRAWN SALAD

Preparation time 25 minutes
Cooking time 15 minutes
To serve 4

You will need

1 small cauliflower
2 pints prawns, peeled
1 green chilli
4 spring onions
½ pint (U.S. 1¼ cups) mayonnaise
½ teaspoon garam masala
a few lettuce leaves
a few coriander leaves

Cut the cauliflower into small flowerets. Boil until tender. Mix the prawns with the cauliflower. Mince the chilli and spring onions finely and blend into the mayonnaise with the garam masala. Combine with the prawns and cauliflower. Prepare a bed of crisp lettuce and pile the salad on top. Sprinkle with coriander leaves and chill before serving.

JINGA TIKKIA

PRAWN CUTLETS

Preparation time 15 minutes
Cooking time 15 minutes
To serve 4

You will need

8 oz. peeled or frozen prawns
1 clove garlic
½-inch fresh root ginger
2 green chillis
1 onion
pinch of chilli powder
pinch of turmeric powder
pinch freshly ground black pepper
1 teaspoon chopped coriander leaves
salt to taste
1 egg
breadcrumbs
butter for frying

Finely mince the prawns, garlic, ginger, chillis and onion and mix with the ground spices, coriander leaves and salt. Mix in the egg and with floured hands shape into flat cutlets. Coat with breadcrumbs and fry.

MASALA MACHI

STUFFED SPICED FISH

(Illustrated in colour on opposite page)

Preparation time 20 minutes
Cooking time 15 minutes
To serve 4

You will need

2 large or 4 small sole
1 dessertspoon ground coriander seeds
1 tablespoon ground cummin seeds
2 cloves garlic, crushed
1 onion, grated
½-inch fresh root ginger, grated
1 teaspoon turmeric powder
salt to taste
water to mix
1 small onion, finely minced
1 green chilli, finely minced
1 tablespoon chopped coriander leaves
oil for frying

FOR THE GARNISH

½ teaspoon carraway seeds
lettuce
2 slices lemon

Clean, trim and wash the fish. Make diagonal cuts, in both directions, 1½ to 2 inches apart on each side of the fish. Combine the next seven ingredients and mix to a paste with a little water. Divide the paste into two portions. To one portion add the onion, chilli and coriander leaves then stuff the fish with it. Rub the remaining paste on to the outside of the fish. Let stand for 1¼ hours. Heat some oil in a frying pan and fry the fish until cooked and brown on both sides. Sprinkle lightly with the caraway seeds and serve on a bed of lettuce. Use lemon slices with a pinch of carraway seeds on each, for garnish.

Stuffed spiced fish

Pickled fish steaks

MACHI MUGARCHEE

PICKLED FISH STEAKS

(Illustrated in colour on opposite page 76)

Preparation time   15 minutes
Cooking time   30 minutes
To serve   4

You will need

8 oz. onions
3 green chillis
2 dry red chillis
1-inch fresh root ginger
1 clove garlic
oil for frying
½ teaspoon turmeric powder
1 tablespoon ground coriander seeds
sprig curry leaves *or*
  2 bay leaves
¼ pint (U.S. ⅔ cup) vinegar
4 thick cod steaks

FOR THE GARNISH

lemon wedges

Finely chop onions, green and red chillis and ginger, crush garlic. Heat the oil in a saucepan and fry onions till golden brown. Add the red chillis, ginger and turmeric and fry for 10 minutes. Add the garlic, green chillis, coriander and curry leaves. Cook for three minutes and add the vinegar. Put in the fish and cook gently till fish is done. Allow to cool in its juices in the refrigerator for 24 hours. Serve cold. Garnish with lemon wedges.

MUSSEL CURRY

Preparation time   15 minutes
Cooking time   30 minutes
To serve   4

You will need

2 quarts mussels
2 large onions
1-inch fresh root ginger
2 cloves garlic
2 green chillis
1 teaspoon turmeric powder
½ teaspoon freshly ground black pepper
3 cloves
oil for frying
½ pint (U.S. 1¼ cups) water
salt to taste

Wash and scrub the mussels thoroughly. Scrape with a sharp knife to remove beards. Finely slice the onions, ginger, garlic and chillis. Mix with the turmeric, black pepper and cloves. Add to the mussels and mix well. Set aside for 10 minutes. Heat some oil in a large saucepan and put in the mussels with all the spices. Fry well for five minutes then add the water and cook gently for about 20 minutes till all the shells have opened.

Mussel curry

JINGA CURRY

HOT PRAWN CURRY

Preparation time   5 minutes
Cooking time   35 minutes
To serve   4

You will need

1 onion
1 clove garlic
oil for frying
1 teaspoon ground cloves
1 tablespoon plain flour
1 teaspoon turmeric powder
2 teaspoons chilli powder
1 teaspoon sugar
1 teaspoon ground cinnamon
$\frac{1}{2}$ pint (U.S. 1$\frac{1}{4}$ cups) beef or chicken stock
2 oz. creamed coconut
16-20 Dublin Bay prawns (according to size)
1 teaspoon lemon juice
salt to taste

Chop the onion finely and crush the garlic. Heat some oil in a saucepan and add onion, garlic and cloves. Fry lightly before adding the flour, turmeric, sugar and cinnamon. Cook gently for a few minutes. Gradually add the stock and coconut to the pan. Bring to the boil, stirring constantly. Reduce heat and simmer for 10 minutes. Add the prawns and lemon juice and season with salt. Cook for another 10 minutes. Serve with chappatis.

Prawn curry

JINGA PALAK

SHRIMPS WITH SPINACH

Preparation time   20 minutes
Cooking time   40 minutes
To serve   4

You will need

1 lb. spinach
2 large onions
1 clove garlic
$\frac{1}{2}$-inch fresh root ginger
2 tomatoes
oil for frying
$\frac{1}{2}$ teaspoon garam masala
$\frac{1}{2}$ teaspoon turmeric powder
$\frac{1}{2}$ teaspoon ground coriander
$\frac{1}{2}$ teaspoon chilli powder
1 teaspoon sugar
salt to taste
1 pint shrimps, picked
FOR THE GARNISH
lemon slices

Wash and chop spinach coarsely. Slice onion, finely; mince garlic and ginger and chop tomatoes. Heat some oil in a pan and fry the onions lightly for five minutes together with the garlic and ginger. Add the spinach and fry for five minutes. Add tomatoes, all the spices and seasonings and simmer for a further 15 minutes. Put in shrimps and continue to cook for 15 minutes. Garnish with lemon slices and serve with chappati or bread.

Shrimps with spinach

JINGA PATIA CURRY

PRAWN CURRY

(Illustrated in colour on page 95)

Preparation time 25 minutes
Cooking time 40 minutes
To serve 4

You will need

1 lb. peeled prawns
salt
8 oz. fresh coriander
2 green chillis
2 dry red chillis
1 lb. onions
oil for frying
1 clove garlic
1 teaspoon ground cummin seeds
½ teaspoon pepper
½ teaspoon turmeric powder
2½ oz. can tomato purée
1 oz. ground tamarind
1 tablespoon flour
½ pint (U.S. 1¼ cups) water

De-vein the prawns and sprinkle with salt. Wash the coriander and pluck the leaves from the stalks. Finely mince the stalks with one green and one red chilli. Combine with the prawns. Now finely mince the onions, remaining chillis, garlic and 1 teaspoon coriander leaves. Brown the onions in some oil. Add the garlic, coriander leaves, cummin, pepper and turmeric and fry for five minutes. Add the prawns, tomato purée and tamarind. Lower the heat and cook for five minutes. Mix flour with enough of the water to make a paste and add to the prawns. Stir in remaining water and cook to thicken, stirring continuously. Serve with rice.

KADU JINGA

COURGETTES WITH PRAWNS

Preparation time 10 minutes
Cooking time 1 hour
To serve 4

You will need

2 onions
2 green chillis
1-inch fresh root ginger
2 cloves garlic
1½ lb. courgettes
oil for frying
1 teaspoon chilli powder
1 teaspoon turmeric powder
½ teaspoon ground cummin seeds
* walnut-sized pece of tamarind, soaked in
   a little hot water
2 teaspoons vinegar
salt to taste
2 teaspoons mollasses
½ pint (U.S. 1¼ cups) water
1 lb. peeled prawns

* Squeeze the husk and strain; use only the water.

Mince the onions, chillis, ginger and garlic. Slice the courgettes into rounds. Heat some oil in a saucepan and fry the onions till brown. Add the chillis, ginger and garlic and fry for a minute or two before adding the chilli powder, turmeric, cummin seeds, tamarind water, vinegar, salt and mollasses. Fry for five minutes and add the water. Continue cooking, uncovered, for 15 minutes before adding the courgettes. Stir, cover and cook for a further 15 minutes. Add the prawns and cook for 10 more minutes.

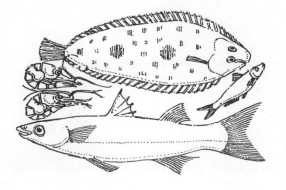

Spiced spinach with hard-boiled eggs

EGGS

In the Indian pattern of dietary habits, eggs are eaten only by non-vegetarians and are generally shunned by others. With the advance of scientific poultry-keeping, unfertilized eggs have gained a measure of popularity and the 'vegetarian egg' is now more acceptable to vegetarians.

The Indian version of scrambled eggs or an omelette has finely minced onion, green chillis, tomatoes and herbs in it — an interesting change from its bland Western counterpart.

Egg curries are usually made with hard-boiled eggs, cooked in a tomato-based gravy. In alternative versions the eggs are poached directly into the curry or are made into small omelettes before being added to the sauce.

It is interesting to note that the Scotch egg has it's counterpart in the Nargis Kabab, see the recipe for Kofta, hard-boiled egg, coated in spiced minced meat, fried and halved.

ANDA DO PIAZA

SPICED SPINACH WITH HARD-BOILED EGGS

Preparation time   15 minutes
Cooking time   40 minutes
To serve   4

You will need

2 large onions
½-inch fresh root ginger
2 cloves garlic
2 tomatoes
2 lb. spinach
oil for frying
2 cloves
1 cardamom seed
1 teaspoon chilli powder
1 teaspoon garam masala
4 hard-boiled eggs
salt to taste

Finely cut onions into rings and mince ginger; crush the garlic and chop the tomatoes. Wash the spinach and cook in a pan till tender, without adding any water. Drain and purée. Heat a little oil and fry the onion, ginger and garlic for two minutes, add cloves and cardamom and fry for another minute. Put in the tomatoes, fry for a further three minutes then add chilli powder and garam masala. Simmer for 15 minutes or until liquid has evaporated.

Stir in the spinach purée and hard-boiled eggs, cut in half. Season with salt and simmer for seven minutes. Serve hot with chappatis.

PARSI BAIDA

EGGS PARSI STYLE

Preparation time 15 minutes
Cooking time 30 minutes
To serve 4

You will need

8 oz. okra
8 onions
2 green chillis
oil for frying
2 tablespoons tomato purée
¼ teaspoon sugar
1 tablespoon chopped coriander
  or parsley leaves
salt to taste
8 eggs

Top and tail the okra. Chop onions and chillis finely.
Heat a little oil and fry onions for two minutes. Add
okra and tomato purée and cook for 15 minutes.
Put in the chillis, sugar, coriander and salt. Remove
and spread mixture in a baking dish. Break the
eggs on top of the okra mixture, cover and bake in
a very moderate oven (300° F — Gas Mark 3)
for 15 minutes or until eggs are set.
Serve with plain boiled rice, garnished with curry
leaves.

DUCK EGGS BALCHOW

SPICED DUCK EGGS

Preparation time 10 minutes
Cooking time 20 minutes
To serve 4

You will need

12 oz. onions
1 clove garlic
1-inch fresh root ginger
2 green chillis
butter for frying
½ teaspoon chilli powder
1 teaspoon ground cummin seeds
1 teaspoon pepper
1 teaspoon turmeric powder
2 bay leaves
salt to taste
8 duck's eggs, beaten

Mince the onions. Mince garlic, ginger and green
chillis finely. Brown onion in a little butter. Add the
ground spices and fry for 2—3 minutes. Add all the
remaining ingredients except the eggs. Cook gently
until the butter floats to the top. Meanwhile,
scramble the eggs in butter in a separate pan and
add to the onions and spices. Cook for a few minutes
and serve with rice or nan.

Eggs Parsee style

Spiced duck eggs

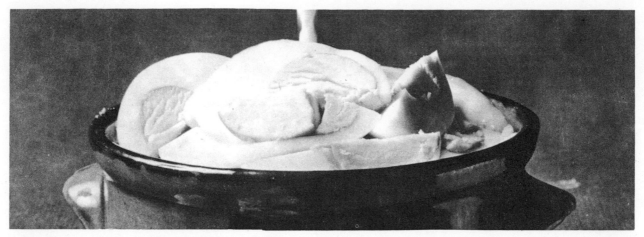

Egg curry

GOA BAIDA CURRY

EGG CURRY

Preparation time   15 minutes
Cooking time   35 minutes
To serve   4

You will need

8 eggs
oil for frying
2 cloves garlic
1 large onion
1 green chilli
1 teaspoon ground coriander seeds
oil for frying
½ teaspoon chilli powder
1 teaspoon poppy seeds
1 teaspoon ground cummin seeds
½-inch slice creamed coconut
3 tablespoons water
* 1 piece tamarind, soaked in
   1 tablespoon hot water
salt to taste

———
* Squeeze and strain the husk, use only the water.

Hard-boil the eggs, peel and deep fry in hot oil till golden brown. Keep aside. Mince the garlic, onion and green chilli. Fry with the coriander in a little oil, for five minutes. Add the chilli powder, poppy and cummin seeds and cook for one minute. Add the coconut and three (U.S. five) tablespoons water, simmer for five minutes. Put in the eggs; add the tamarind liquid and the salt. Cook for 20 minutes. Serve with rice.

MOOTAY MOLEE

EGG CURRY IN COCONUT MILK

Preparation time   10 minutes
Cooking time   30 minutes
To serve   4

You will need

oil for frying
1 large onion, finely sliced
2 cloves garlic, crushed
1-inch fresh root ginger, finely minced
4 green chillis, slit lengthwise
4 cloves
1-inch stick cinnamon
1 level teaspoon turmeric powder
10 oz. thick coconut milk (see page 7)
salt to taste
6 hard-boiled eggs

Heat some oil in a saucepan and lightly fry the onion. Add the garlic, ginger, chillis, cloves and cinnamon. Fry for 2—3 minutes. Add turmeric and cook for a further two minutes. Add coconut milk and salt, bring to the boil then simmer uncovered, until gravy is thick. Cut eggs in half lengthwise and add to gravy, heat throughly and serve.

NARIEL ANDA CURRY

COCONUT EGG CURRY

(Illustrated in colour on opposite page)

Preparation time   15 minutes
Cooking time   35 minutes
To serve   4

You will need

1 lb. tomatoes
½ pint (U.S. 1¼ cups) water
1 large onion
1 clove garlic
oil for frying
1 tablespoon ground almonds
1 teaspoon chilli powder
1 teaspoon turmeric powder
1 teaspoon ground coriander seeds
¼ teaspoon ground ginger
2 oz. creamed coconut
1 bay leaf
1 dessertspoon gram flour
  or cornflour
salt to taste
6-8 hard-boiled eggs

Cook tomatoes in the water for a few minutes or till soft. Drain, pass through a sieve and set aside. Slice onion and crush garlic. Heat a little oil and fry onion till brown. Add almonds, chilli powder, turmeric, coriander, ginger and garlic. Fry, stirring, till well browned. Put in sieved tomatoes, coconut and bay leaf and bring to the boil. Stir in the gram flour and lower heat. Season with salt and simmer gently for 30 minutes till thickened. If too thick add a little more water. Halve and add the eggs. Cook for five minutes more and serve with nan or roti.

PORA

BAKED EGGS WITH SHRIMPS

Preparation time   15 minutes
Cooking time   20 minutes
To serve   4

You will need

2 green chillis
1 bunch coriander leaves
2 cloves garlic
½-inch fresh root ginger
½ teaspoon ground cummin seeds
pinch of turmeric powder
10 egg whites
5 egg yolks
2 teaspoons flour
salt to taste
4 oz. peeled shrimps
knob of butter

Very finely mince the chillis, coriander leaves, garlic and ginger and mix with ground cummin and turmeric powder. Put egg whites in a mixing bowl and whisk till stiff, add egg yolks and beat again. Stir in the flour and add the spices, salt and shrimps. Heat the butter in a frying pan and pour in egg mixture. Cook, stirring quickly, till slightly thickened. Then pour into a baking dish and bake in a moderate oven (350° F. — Gas Mark 4) for 15 minutes or till set. Serve with puris (see page 132) or cut into strips and roll in chappatis (see page 136).

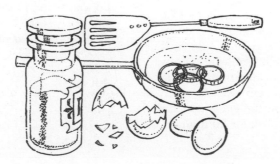

Coconut egg curry

Chicken pulao and stuffed peppers

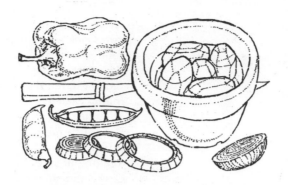

VEGETABLES

To be a vegetarian in India is not a deprivation for there is an abundance of vegetables throughour the year. Because of the several varieties of vegetables and the many different ways of cooking them, vegetarian food is interesting and exciting. The humble potato is boiled, fried, stuffed and curried in endless ways — it is even served as a delectable sweet. Vegetable Curry, for example, can be one or more vegetables, cooked with spices in a gravy. When the vegetables are cooked with spices but without liquid and served dry, the dish is called a 'bhujia'. 'Foogath' are spiced vegetables cooked with coconut, but if the vegetables are cooked and then added to the spices and coconut without any further cooking the dish is called a 'sambal' and, as other vegetable dishes, it is served as an accompaniment to a meal. So too is 'raita' in which the vegetables are chopped and mixed with yoghurt. If a vegetable is roasted and mashed before being mixed with spices it is called a 'bhartha'. Besides these dishes there are vegetable koftas — made of mashed vegetables, formed into balls and put into curries. Dhals, or pulses, are among the most popular dishes throughout India; eaten at every meal they are tasty, cheap and nutritious.

Paneer or Indian cream cheese is often cooked with vegetables or added just before serving to make tasty dishes. A recipe for making it can be found at the beginning of this chapter.

MIRCHI BHARWAN

STUFFED PEPPERS

(Illustrated in colour on opposite page)

Preparation time   15 minutes
Cooking time   50 minutes
To serve   4

You will need

8 medium-sized peppers
1 lb. minced beef
3 oz. rice
1 onion, finely chopped
1 dessertspoon ground coriander seeds
½ teaspoon chilli powder
1 teaspoon sugar

grated rind of 1 lemon and
  juice of ½ lemon
salt to taste
1 tablespoon oil
Stock

Wash and dry peppers. Cut a slice from the base of each one, leaving the stalks intact; remove seeds. Mix all the other ingredients, except oil and stock, together in a bowl. Blend thoroughly and use to stuff the peppers — do not stuff too tightly as the rice will swell during cooking. Heat some oil in a large saucepan, place the peppers upright and fry for a few seconds then add stock to come half way up the peppers. Cover pan and simmer gently for 45 minutes. Alternatively, bake in a moderate oven (350° F. — Gas Mark 4) for 1½ hours. Serve either hot or cold.

GOBI BHARWAN

STUFFED CABBAGE LEAVES

Preparation time   10 minutes
Cooking time   40-45 minutes
To serve   4

You will need

8 large cabbage leaves
1 small onion
2 cloves garlic
2-inch fresh root ginger
2 green chillis
1 dessertspoon coriander leaves
oil for frying
12 oz. potatoes, boiled and roughly mashed
1 oz. sultanas
¼ teaspoon chilli powder
salt to taste
juice of ½ lemon

FOR THE SAUCE

oil for frying
2¼ oz. can tomato purée
5 tablespoons water
salt to taste
pinch of chilli powder

Blanch the cabbage leaves in salted boiling water. Drain and cool.
Finely chop the onion, garlic, ginger, chillis and coriander leaves. Heat some oil in a pan and lightly fry the onion and garlic. Add the potatoes, ginger,

Vegetable curry (2)

chillis, coriander leaves, sultanas, chilli powder and salt. Cook for 10 minutes then add lemon juice and cool. Divide mixture into eight equal portions. If the stalks of the cabbage leaves are coarse, remove them. Flatten the leaves and stuff with the mixture, rolling each leaf like a small parcel. Tie with thread or secure with cocktail sticks.
Put a little oil in a large saucepan, when hot add the cabbage rolls. Cook for a few seconds, before adding tomato purée with the water, salt and chilli powder. Cover and simmer for about 30 minutes.

SABZI KA CURRY

VEGETABLE CURRY (1)

Preparation time   15 minutes
Cooking time   45 minutes
To serve   4

You will need

8 oz. potatoes
4 oz. carrots
4 oz. turnip
4 oz. runner beans
4 oz. shelled peas
1 large onion, sliced finely
oil for frying
1 clove garlic
1 tablespoon ground coriander seeds
1½ teaspoons chilli powder
1 teaspoon turmeric powder
1 teaspoon ground ginger
½ teaspoon ground cummin seeds
½ teaspoon ground mustard seeds
2¼ oz. can tomato purée
water to mix
½ oz. creamed coconut
salt to taste
squeeze of lemon juice

Chop the potatoes, carrots, and beans, then parboil with the peas. Now fry the onion in a little oil and when golden brown add the garlic. After a minute or two add all the spices and fry briskly. Add the tomato purée and a little water to make a thick gravy. Lower the heat, cover the pan and simmer gently for 20 minutes. Add the creamed coconut, vegetables and salt and cook till vegetables are tender. Add lemon juice to taste.

GOODA AUR SABZI KA CURRY

VEGETABLE CURRY (2)

Preparation time 5 minutes
Cooking time 50 minutes
To serve 4

You will need

2 onions
3 aubergines
4 large tomatoes
oil for frying
1 teaspoon aniseed
pinch of ground cinnamon
sprig of curry leaves
1 teaspoon chilli powder
½ tablespoon ground coriander seeds
pinch turmeric powder
12 pieces marrow bone,
    chopped into 3-inch lengths
few sprigs cauliflower
1 red pepper, sliced
salt to taste

Slice onions and aubergines and chop tomatoes. Heat some oil in a saucepan and fry the aniseed and cinnamon for a minute or two before adding the onions and curry leaves. When the onion turns brown add the chilli powder, coriander and turmeric. Cook for five minutes and add tomatoes. Cook till pulpy. Add the bones, aubergines, cauliflower and pepper. Season with salt and simmer gently until the vegetables are tender. Serve hot with chappatis.

If desired, or when aubergines are not in season or are unobtainable, potatoes may be substituted. Slice them evenly and follow the method given above.

PANEER

INDIAN CREAM CHEESE

Preparation time 3 minutes
Cooking time 7 minutes
To make 6 oz. cheese

You will need

2 pints (U.S. 5 cups) milk
1 teaspoon salt
2 cartons yoghurt

Bring milk to the boil and add salt. Remove from the heat and mix the yoghurt into it. Stir gently till all the milk curdles. Place butter muslin over a colander and pour the curdled milk into it. Draw up the corners of the muslin and squeeze gently. Shape the cheese into a round or rectangle and place a weight on it (a saucepan filled with water can be used). Leave for 1½ hours.

To cook, cut into small cubes or rectangles and deep fry to a golden brown. Fry carefully as the paneer tends to catch and burn. Add to various vegetable dishes before serving.

Paneer

PAKORA CURRY

FRIED BATTER BALL CURRY

Preparation time   15 minutes
Cooking time   1 hour
To serve   4

You will need

FOR THE PAKORAS

8 oz. gram flour
salt to taste
¼ pint (U.S. ⅔ cup) water
1 onion
1 green chilli
oil for deep frying

FOR THE CURRY

1 small onion
2 cloves garlic
2 tomatoes
1 large potato
oil for frying
1 teaspoon mustard seed
1 tablespoon dessicated coconut, soaked in
  2 tablespoons milk
1 teaspoon turmeric powder
1 teaspoon ground coriander seeds
½ teaspoon chilli powder
½ pint (U.S. 1¼ cup) water

Sieve flour and salt into a basin. Beat in the water to make a batter. Slice the onion and chilli and mix into batter. Heat some oil in a deep pan and fry spoonfuls of the batter till golden brown. Drain and set aside.
For the curry, mince the onion and garlic finely; chop tomatoes and peel and dice potato. Heat a little oil in a saucepan and fry the mustard seeds until they stop spluttering. Add the onion, garlic, strained coconut milk, turmeric, coriander and chilli powder and fry for seven minutes. Add water and simmer for 15 minutes before adding tomatoes and potato. Simmer till the potato is nearly cooked. Add the pakoras and simmer gently for a further 15 minutes. Garnish with either desiccated coconut or fresh coriander leaves.

ALOO MIRCHI

GREEN PEPPERS STUFFED WITH POTATO

Preparation time   15 minutes
Cooking time   45 minutes
To serve   4

You will need

4 large green peppers
4 large potatoes
2 tomatoes
2 medium-sized onions
oil for frying
1 tablespoon chopped peanuts
1 teaspoon chilli powder
½ teaspoon garam masala
½ teaspoon ground cummin seeds
1 teaspoon pomegranate seeds (optional)
salt to taste
2 tablespoons grated parmesan cheese

Halve the peppers lengthways and remove pith and seeds. Dip in boiling water for a minute to soften. Set aside. Boil the potatoes, peel and mash coarsely. Chop tomatoes and slice onions. Heat some oil in a pan and fry the onions till translucent. Add tomatoes and nuts and fry for a minute. Put in the spices and salt to taste and cook for five minutes. Add the potatoes and fry for five minutes. Stuff the potato mixture into the halved peppers. Sprinkle the cheese on top. Grill for 10 minutes.

Green peppers stuffed with potato

Yoghurt with mango

AM RAITHA

YOGHURT WITH MANGO

Preparation time 10 minutes
Cooking time 5 minutes
To serve 4

You will need

3 ripe mangoes *or*
 1 × 32 oz. can of mangoes
¼ teaspoon mustard seeds
oil or ghee for frying
2 green chillis
2 cloves garlic
2 cartons yoghurt
salt to taste
pinch of sugar

Peel the fresh mangoes, chop coarsely and set aside. If using canned ones, drain. Fry the mustard seeds in a little oil or ghee until they begin to splutter. Finely mince the green chillis and garlic and add to the mangoes along with the mustard seeds, yoghurt, salt and sugar.

GOBI KA FOOGATH

SPICED CABBAGE

Preparation time 5 minutes
Cooking time 30 minutes
To serve 4

You will need

1 large cabbage
1 large onion, finely sliced
2 cloves garlic, crushed
oil for frying
1-inch fresh root ginger, finely sliced
2-3 green chillis, slit
1 heaped tablespoon desiccated coconut
salt to taste

Shred the cabbage roughly. Now fry the onion and garlic in a little oil and when soft and transparent add the ginger and chillis. Fry for a few minutes before adding the cabbage. Stir well, cover the pan and lower the heat. Cook about 15 minutes. Add coconut and salt. Stir well and cook 5 minutes more.

AM KA CURRY

RIPE MANGO CURRY

Preparation time 10 minutes
Cooking time 30 minutes
To serve 4

You will need

4 medium-sized mangoes
water
½ teaspoon turmeric powder
½ teaspoon chilli powder
2 green chillis
1 pint buttermilk
2 oz. creamed coconut
salt to taste
oil for frying
1 teaspoon mustard seeds
small bunch curry leaves
 or 2 bay leaves
2 dry red chillis

Peel the mangoes and cut into quarters. Put into a pan with the stones and a little water. Add turmeric and chilli powder and simmer till mangoes are tender. Meanwhile mince the green chillis finely and add to the mangoes along with the buttermilk, coconut and salt. Bring to the boil and remove from the heat. In a small pan fry the mustard seeds, curry leaves and dry chillis. Add to the curry and serve with plain boiled rice.

BUND GOBI BHAJI

CURRIED CABBAGE

Preparation time   10 minutes
Cooking time   25 minutes
To serve   4

You will need

1 lb. firm cabbage
8 oz. potatoes
oil for frying
1 tablespoon mustard seeds
¼ teaspoon fenugreek seeds
½-inch slice creamed coconut
½ teaspoon chilli powder
salt to taste

Shred cabbage, scrub potatoes and dice without removing the skin. Heat a little oil in a pan and fry the mustard and fenugreek seeds until they seeds splutter. Put in the cabbage and coconut. Stir and cook for 2 minutes. Add potatoes, chilli powder and salt. Simmer until cooked.

Curried cabbage

cabbage. Stir well, cover with a lid and simmer gently till cooked. Be careful not to overcook.

GOBI MIRCHA

CABBAGE WITH GREEN PEPPERS

Preparation time   10 minutes
Cooking time   30 minutes
To serve   4

You will need

1 cabbage (at least 2 lb.)
1 large onion
2 large green peppers
2 green chillis
oil for frying
1 teaspoon turmeric powder
salt to taste

Shred cabbage, slice onion, chop green peppers and mince chillis. Fry the onion in a little oil until golden. Add chillis and fry for two minutes then add the peppers and fry for five minutes. Add turmeric and salt and cook for one minute before adding the

BRINJAL BHARTA

SPICED PURÉE OF AUBERGINE

Preparation time   10 minutes
Cooking time   45 minutes
To serve   4

You will need

1 large aubergine (approximately 1 lb.)
3 spring onions
1 dessertspoon coriander leaves
2 cloves garlic
2 green chillis
¼ teaspoon cummin seeds
2 cartons yoghurt
salt to taste
1 tablespoon ghee or oil

Cut the aubergine in half lengthways. Cover with foil and bake in a moderate oven (350° F. — Gas Mark 4) for 40 minutes or until tender. Remove the skin and mash the flesh of the aubergine. Finely mince the onions, coriander leaves, garlic and green chillis and add to the aubergine along with the yoghurt and salt. Heat the ghee or oil in a saucepan and add the mixture. Heat through.

Cauliflower masala curry

Baked spiced cauliflower

GOBI MASALA

CAULIFLOWER MASALA CURRY

Preparation time   10 minutes
Cooking time   25 minutes
To serve   4

You will need

* walnut-sized piece of tamarind, soaked in
  2 tablespoons boiling water
1 tablespoon gram flour
½ teaspoon chilli powder
1 teaspoon ground coriander seeds
1 cauliflower
¼-inch slice creamed coconut, dissolved in
  5 tablespoons milk
1 teaspoon mustard seeds
oil for frying
salt to taste

* Squeeze the husk and strain;
use only the water.

Combine the tamarind water with the gram flour,
chilli powder and coriander, in a saucepan. Break
the cauliflower into sprigs and add to the ingredients in the pan with the coconut milk. Fry the
mustard seeds in a little oil until they begin to
splutter. Add to the cauliflower. Season with salt.
Cover with a lid and simmer gently until the cauliflower is tender. If necessary add a little water.

DUM GOBI

BAKED SPICED CAULIFLOWER

Preparation time   10 minutes
Cooking time   2 hours
To serve   4

You will need

1 cauliflower (approximately 1½ lb.)
1 onion
2 cartons yoghurt
2 tablespoons tomato purée
1 teaspoon ground coriander seeds
¼ teaspoon chilli powder
½ teaspoon garam masala
¼ teaspoon ground ginger
salt to taste
little melted butter

Trim the cauliflower. Mince the onion finely and
mix with the yoghurt, tomato purée, coriander,
chilli powder, garam masala and ginger. Mix well
and season with salt. Place the cauliflower in a deep
casserole and cover it with the spice mixture. Bake
in a moderate oven (375° — Gas Mark 5) for
2 hours. Baste occasionally with the sauce. Half
way through the cooking time brush with a little
melted butter. If the cauliflower becomes too dry
cover the casserole with foil.

Masala Aubergine

MASALA BENGAN

MASALA AUBERGINE

Preparation time 15 minutes
Cooking time 25 minutes
To serve 4

You will need

4 aubergines
3 green chillis
1 onion
1-inch fresh root ginger
oz. creamed coconut
½ pint water
2 tablespoons vinegar
salt to taste

Core the aubergines, and simmer in a little water until tender. Cut into wedges. Skin the onion. Mince or grate the chillis, onion and the fresh root ginger as finely as possible, then mix with the aubergine along with the creamed coconut. Gradually add the water and simmer for approximately 7 minutes, stirring occasionally. Add the vinegar and the salt, stir well and serve hot.

BAGARA BENGAN

CURRIED AUBERGINE

(Illustrated in colour on page 96)

Preparation time 15 minutes
Cooking time 55 minutes
To serve 4

You will need

1 lb. aubergines
oil for frying
4 large onions, sliced
1 teaspoon ground coriander seeds
2 green chillis
½ teaspoon chilli powder
½-inch slice creamed coconut
2 cloves garlic, crushed
1 teaspoon turmeric powder
* 4 oz. tamarind, soaked in
   ¼ pint (U.S. ⅔ cup) water
1 dessertspoon ground gingelly
   or sesame seeds
1 tablespoon molasses
1 teaspoon mustard seeds
A few curry leaves
   or bay leaves
salt to taste

———

* Squeeze the husk and strain, use only the water.

Wash the aubergines and without removing the stalks, cut lengthways into quarters. Heat some oil in a heavy frying pan and fry the aubergines until the skins turn brown. Remove from the pan and set aside. Heat some more oil in a saucepan and fry onions until soft; add coriander and the chillis. Fry for two minutes; add the chilli powder, coconut, garlic and turmeric then fry for a further five minutes. Add the tamarind water, gingelly or sesame seeds, molasses and aubergine. Cover with a tight-fitting lid and cook gently until aubergines are tender. Meanwhile fry the mustard seeds and curry leaves until the seeds crackle. Combine with the aubergine and season with salt.

Prawn curry

Curried aubergine and okra curry

BHENDI RAITHA (1)

YOGHURT WITH OKRA

Preparation time	5 minutes
Cooking time	20 minutes
To serve	4

You will need

8 oz. okra
2 green chillis
1-inch fresh root ginger
1 dessertspoon fresh coriander leaves
oil for frying
½ teaspoon turmeric powder
5 cartons yoghurt
salt to taste

FOR THE GARNISH

coriander leaves

Slice okra into rings. Mince chillis, ginger and coriander leaves. Heat some oil in a pan and fry okra for five minutes. Add turmeric and salt and fry for a further two minutes before adding chillis and ginger. Continue cooking gently till okra is tender. Meanwhile put yoghurt in a bowl and beat well with salt. Add to the okra, mix and garnish with coriander leaves.

BHENDI RAITHA (2)

YOGHURT WITH OKRA

Preparation time	10 minutes
Cooking time	25 minutes
To serve	4

You will need

oil for frying
1 lb. okra, cut in half
salt to taste
1 teaspoon turmeric powder
1-inch fresh root ginger, finely minced
1½ cartons yoghurt
1 heaped tablespoon desiccated coconut, soaked in
  1 tablespoon hot water
1 teaspoon fresh coriander leaves, chopped

Heat some oil in a saucepan and fry the okra for five minutes. Add salt, turmeric and ginger and fry well for 10 minutes, till okra is cooked. Beat the yoghurt with the coconut, chilli powder and coriander leaves. Add to the okra, bring to the boil, lower heat and simmer for a few minutes.

BHENDI CURRY

OKRA CURRY

(Illustrated in colour on opposite page)

Preparation time	15 minutes
Cooking time	45 minutes
To serve	4

You will need

1 lb. okra
2 onions
2 green chillis
1 clove garlic
1-inch fresh root ginger
oil for frying
1 tablespoon ground coriander
1 teaspoon turmeric powder
* 2 oz. tamarind, soaked for 30 minutes in
   8 tablespoons boiling water
1½ oz. creamed coconut
2 tomatoes, quartered
salt to taste

* Squeeze the husk and discard. Strain the liquid.

Top and tail okra, wash and cut in half. Finely, mince onions separately, then mince the green chillis, garlic and ginger. Heat some oil in a saucepan and fry onions till brown. Add chillis, garlic and ginger and fry for another three minutes. Add coriander and turmeric and fry well. Now add tamarind water and coconut, bring to the boil, lower heat and simmer for 30 minutes. Add okra and tomatoes, season with salt, and cook for a further 5—10 minutes.

BHINDANI KADHI

OKRA COOKED IN BUTTERMILK

Preparation time   10 minutes
Cooking time   35-40 minutes
To serve   4

You will need

oil for frying
1 lb. okra, sliced
1 teaspoon turmeric powder
1-inch fresh root ginger, finely chopped
2 green chillis, finely chopped
pinch of salt
1 level dessertspoon besan (gram flour)
½ pint (U.S. 1¼ cups) buttermilk
2 teaspoons chopped coriander leaves

Heat some oil in a saucepan and fry the okra gently. When well fried add the turmeric, ginger, chillis, and salt. Fry till the raw smell of the turmeric has gone and add the gram flour. Fry for a minute or two and add the buttermilk gradually, stirring constantly. Bring to the boil, lower heat and simmer for few minutes. Sprinkle with coriander leaves.

Carrot and nut curry

Chop the onions and cut the carrots into quarters. Chop the tomato then finely mince the chilli. Fry the onions gently in a little oil until transparent. Add the flour, stir and cook for one minute before adding the fenugreek and tomato then cook for a further two minutes. Put in the carrots and nuts, stir and add the garam masala, chilli and ginger. Pour in the milk, stir until thickened then add salt. Cover and simmer gently, stirring occasionally, until carrots are tender.

GAJJAR KAJU CURRY

CARROT AND NUT CURRY

Preparation time   10 minutes
Cooking time   30 minutes
To serve   4

You will need

2 onions
12 oz. carrots
1 tomato
1 green chilli
oil for frying
1 teaspoon flour
¼ teaspoon fenugreek (optional)
12 oz. cashew nuts
½ teaspoon garam masala
¼ teaspoon ground ginger
scant ¼ pint (U.S. ½ cup) milk
salt to taste

CHINGRI SAMBAL

SPICED COURGETTE

Preparation time   20 minutes
Cooking time   30 minutes
To serve   4

You will need

1 lb. courgettes
oil for frying
1 onion
1 teaspoon crushed dried prawns
2 teaspoons chilli powder
* ¼ oz. tamarind, soaked in
  1 tablespoon hot water
¼-inch slice creamed coconut
salt to taste

---

* Soak tamarind in hot water for 20 minutes. Squeeze the husk and strain the liquid.

Slice the courgettes and fry in a little oil until golden. Drain and set aside. Slice the onion and fry along with the crushed prawns until soft. Add the chilli powder, courgettes, tamarind water, coconut and salt. Cook for 20 minutes, stirring constantly. Serve with rice.

Celery doroo

CELERY DOROO

SPICED CELERY

Preparation time 15 minutes
Cooking time 40 minutes
To serve 4

You will need

2 heads celery
little water
1 onion
1 clove garlic
½-inch fresh root ginger
oil for frying
½ teaspoon ground cummin seeds
½ teaspoon chilli powder
1 teaspoon desiccated coconut
½ teaspoon ground coriander seeds
1 teaspoon molasses
* ½ pint (U.S. 1¼ cups) tamarind water
1 oz. creamed coconut
salt to taste
2 teaspoons chopped coriander leaves

* Soak a 1-inch piece of tamarind in hot water. When the tamarind becomes pulpy, squeeze and discard it.

Wash celery and cut into 4-inch pieces. Simmer until tender and set aside. Slice onion, crush garlic and mince ginger. Fry the onion to a golden brown. Add cummin seeds, chilli powder, garlic, ginger and desiccated coconut, fry for three minutes. Then add the ground coriander seeds, the freshly chopped coriander leaves, molasses, tamarind water, creamed coconut, and salt. Bring to the boil, add the celery and simmer for 10 minutes.

Chingri sambal

DOODHI BHAJI

CURRIED MARROW

Preparation time 10 minutes
Cooking time 35 minutes
To serve 4

You will need

1 young marrow (approximately 1½ lb.)
2 onions
2 tomatoes, peeled
1 teaspoon mustard seeds
oil for frying
1 teaspoon garam masala
½ teaspoon turmeric powder
½ teaspoon chilli powder
salt to taste
¼-inch slice creamed coconut

Peel the marrow, cut in half, remove seeds then dice into 1-inch cubes. Finely slice the onions and chop tomatoes. Fry mustard seeds in a little oil until they splutter, then add the onions and fry till tender and transparent. Add tomatoes together with the garam masala, turmeric and chilli powder and fry for five minutes. Add marrow and salt to taste. Simmer for five minutes before adding the coconut. Cover and cook for a further 10 minutes. Serve with tomato wedges.

PANEER MATAR

PEAS AND CREAM CHEESE

Preparation time 10 minutes
Cooking time 30 minutes
To serve 4

You will need

6 oz. prepared paneer (see page 89)
oil for frying
1 onion
2 tomatoes
1 green chilli
1-inch fresh root ginger
* 1 lb. peas (shelled)
salt to taste

FOR THE GARNISH

1 teaspoon chopped coriander leaves

* If frozen peas are used, fry all the ingredients first and cook for 20 minutes then add the peas.

Dice the paneer and fry in a little oil till golden brown. Drain the paneer and set aside. Mince the onion, chop tomatoes, finely chop chilli and ginger. Fry the onion until soft. Add the chilli and ginger and cook for 1—2 minutes. Add the shelled peas and remaining ingredients. Simmer until the peas are tender. Stir in the paneer. Sprinkle with coriander leaves and serve hot.

Curried marrow

MATAR KOFTA CURRY

CURRIED PEA FRITTERS

Preparation time 15 minutes
Cooking time 1 hour
To serve 4

You will need

2 lb. peas
1 teaspoon poppy seeds
gram flour to bind
oil for frying
1 onion
2 large potatoes
1 teaspoon ground cloves
1 teaspoon ground cummin seeds
½ teaspoon turmeric powder
1 teaspoon garam masala
salt to taste

Shell and boil the green peas then mash them. Mix
with the poppy seeds and add sufficient gram flour
to make a stiff paste. Mould into balls and fry till
golden brown. Drain and set aside. Mince onion
finely and peel and cube potatoes. Fry the spices
in a little oil until the raw smell disappears. Add the
onions and fry until brown. Add the potatoes and
a little water and cook till tender. Season with salt
and add the pea koftas before serving. Serve with
a salad.

Curried pea fritters

Peas and cream cheese

MATAR AUR ANDA KA CURRY

EGG AND GREEN PEA CURRY

Preparation time 10 minutes
Cooking time 45 minutes
To serve 4

You will need

1 large onion, finely minced
oil for frying
1 clove garlic, crushed
1 teaspoon turmeric powder
1 teaspoon chilli powder
1 teaspoon ground ginger
2 teaspoons ground coriander seeds
2½ oz. can tomato purée
salt to taste
1 pint (U.S. 2½ cups) water
1 oz. creamed coconut
8 oz. shelled peas
6 hard-boiled eggs, cut in halves lengthwise

Fry the onion in some oil until golden brown. Add
garlic, fry for two minutes and add the spices. Fry
well before adding the tomato purée, salt and water.
Cook till gravy begins to thicken then add the
coconut and when dissolved add the peas and eggs.
Cook for another 10 minutes.

MATTAR GUCHI

SPICED PEAS AND MUSHROOMS

Preparation time 10 minutes
Cooking time 30 minutes
To serve 4

You will need

8 oz. mushrooms, washed and trimmed
2 onions
1 clove garlic
1 tomato
oil for fryig
8 oz. shelled peas
½ teaspoon turmeric powder
½ teaspoon garam masala
½ teaspoon chilli powder
salt to taste

Cut mushrooms in slices. Slice onions finely, crush garlic, and peel and chop tomato. Fry the onions in a little oil until pale gold. Add garlic and tomato and mix well. Put in the turmeric, garam masala, chilli powder and mushrooms. Stir and fry for five minutes. Season with salt and simmer until mushrooms are tender, adding a very little water if necessary.

MATAR KHORMA

PEAS IN TOMATO PURÉE

Preparation time 10 minutes
Cooking time 20 minutes
To serve 4

You will need

1 lb. ripe tomatoes
8 oz. young peas (shelled)
½-inch fresh root ginger
2 green chillis
oil for frying
½ teaspoon garam masala

Put the tomatoes in a bowl. Pour boiling water over them and leave for 20 seconds. Peel and mash the tomatoes to a purée. Boil the peas and ad to the

Spiced peas and mushrooms

purée. Finely mince the ginger and chillis and add to the tomatoes and peas. Heat some oil in a pan, add the tomatoes and peas and cook for 15 minutes over a low heat. Sprinkle with the garam masala and serve with plain boiled rice and papadoms.

MAHASHA

STUFFED ONIONS

Preparation time 25 minutes
Cooking time 1 hour
To serve 4-6

Peas in tomato purée

You will need

6 very large onions
1 tablespoon oil

FOR THE FILLING

1 lb. veal or chicken, minced
3 oz. rice
grated peel and juice of 1 lemon
2 tomatoes, skinned and chopped
1 small onion, finely chopped
1 dessertspoon sugar
seasoning
1 teaspoon turmeric powder

Parboil the onions in their skins and when cool but not cold, slit each onion with a sharp knife, down one side to the centre. Remove outer skin and now slip each successive layer off.

Mix the ingredients for the filling. Take a small handful of the mixture, squeeze to make a sausage shape and stuff each onion skin carefully, rolling the skin tightly around to enclose the mixture. Keep any juice that remains from the mixture. Heat the oil in a deep pan and place onions in it, close together. Pour in the left-over juice and simmer very gently for 45 minutes. By this time the liquid will have evaporated and the onions will be brown on one side, turn them over carefully and when they are brown on the other side they are ready to serve either hot or cold.

BHUNA ALOO

SPICED FRIED POTATOES

Preparation time 3 minutes
Cooking time 20 minutes
To serve 4

You will need

1 lb. small new potatoes
pomegranate seeds (optional)
1 teaspoon garam masala
1 teaspoon chillli powder
salt to taste
oil for frying
chopped parsley

Wash the potatoes but do not peel. Rub them with the pomegranate seeds if used, garam masala, chilli

powder and salt. Heat some oil in a large shallow frying pan and fry the potatoes until cooked, drain well. Sprinkle with the chopped parsley and serve very hot. If preferred the potatoes can be deep fried.

ALOO FOOGATH

POTATOES WITH ONIONS

Preparation time 10 minutes
Cooking time 30 minutes
To serve 4

You will need

2 lb. potatoes
12 oz. onion
2 cloves garlic
1-inch fresh root ginger
$\frac{1}{4}$ teaspoon ground cloves
$\frac{3}{4}$ teaspoon ground cinnamon
$\frac{1}{4}$ teaspoon turmeric powder
oil for frying
salt to taste

Peel and chop the potatoes and onions roughly. Crush the garlic and finely mince the ginger. Fry the garlic, ginger, cloves, cinnamon and turmeric in oil for five minutes. Add the onions and fry for five minutes. Add potatoes and salt and cook until potatoes are soft. Serve with nan and yoghurt.

Potatoes with onions

ALU BHAJI

SPICED POTATOES

Preparation time   5 minutes
Cooking time   25 minutes
To serve   4

You will need

1 lb. potatoes
2 green chillis
1 teaspoon mustard seeds
oil for frying
1 teaspoon turmeric powder
salt to taste
1 teaspoon sugar
lemon juice

FOR THE GARNISH

Few coriander leaves

Cube and boil potatoes. Chop chillis and coriander leaves. Fry mustard seeds in a little oil and when they stop spluttering put in the turmeric. Stir once and then quickly add potatoes, chillis and salt. Fry for 1—2 minutes then add sugar and lemon juice. Fry for a few minutes to brown. Serve garnished with coriander leaves.

ALU PALAK

SPINACH WITH POTATOES

Preparation time   15 minutes
Cooking time   35 minutes
To serve   4

You will need

2 lb. spinach
12 oz. potatoes
2 large onions
2 green chillis
oil for frying
1 teaspoon turmeric powder
1 teaspoon mustard seeds
1 teaspoon chilli powder
salt to taste
1 teaspoon sugar

Wash spinach thoroughly, squeeze to get rid of the water, chop roughly. Cube potatoes and par-boil. Slice onions and chop chillis. Now heat some oil in a saucepan and put in turmeric, mustard seeds and chilli powder. Fry till the mustard seeds pop, add the potatoes, onions, chillis and salt. Fry well for about 10 minutes and add the spinach and sugar. Stir well and simmer covered till spinach and potatoes are cooked. Uncover and cook to evaporate the liquid.

MASALA MULI

SPICED RADISHES

Preparation time   20 minutes
Cooking time   50 minutes
To serve   4

You will need

1 lb. white radishes
2 large onions
oil for frying
2 tablespoons desiccated coconut, soaked in
   2 tablespoons milk
$\frac{1}{4}$ teaspoon ground cloves
$\frac{1}{2}$ teaspoon black pepper
1 teaspoon ground coriander
1 teaspoon chilli powder
1 teaspoon garam masala
$\frac{1}{2}$ teaspoon turmeric powder
salt to taste
water to blend

Prepare the radishes, cutting them into quarters and put them in a saucepan; mince the onions finely and fry them in a little oil until brown. Do not allow to burn. Squeeze the coconut and discard. Add the milk to the pan with the cloves, black pepper, coriander, chilli powder, garam masala, turmeric powder and salt to taste. Fry for 10 minutes. Blend with a little water and add to the radishes. Cook gently until the radishes are tender and the gravy thickens. Serve with chappatis or bread.

Spiced radishes

DAHI ALOO

POTATOES WITH YOGHURT

Preparation time   15 minutes
Cooking time   40 minutes
To serve   4

You will need

1 lb. small potatoes
oil for frying
2 onions
½-inch fresh root ginger
2 green chillis
2 tomatoes
2 teaspoons ground coriander seeds
1 teaspoon turmeric powder
1 teaspoon garam masala
2 cartons yoghurt
1 oz. raisins
salt to taste
½ teaspoon chilli powder
1 teaspoon sugar

FOR THE GARNISH

1 tablespoon chopped coriander leaves

Boil potatoes in salted water. When cooked drain, peel and fry in oil until slightly brown. Drain and set aside. Chop the onions finely; mince the ginger and chillis very finely and chop the tomatoes. Heat some more oil and fry the onions until soft but not brown. Add the ginger, ground coriander, turmeric and garam masala and fry for five minutes. Add chillis, tomatoes and yoghurt. Stir until the sauce is beginning to thicken, then add the raisins, salt and chilli powder. Simmer until the gravy is thick. Add the potatoes and sugar and cook for a minute or two. Serve hot, garnished with chopped coriander leaves.

BHENDI BATATA

POTATOES WITH OKRA

Preparation time   10 minutes
Cooking time   40 minutes
To serve   4

You will need

12 oz. potatoes, cut into cubes
12 oz. okra
1 onion, sliced
2 green chillis
oil for frying
1 teaspoon turmeric powder
½ teaspoon chilli powder
salt to taste
a little water

FOR THE GARNISH

1 dessertspoon coriander leaves, chopped
1 teaspoon grated coconut

Cube the potatoes, chop the okra, slice the onions and slit the chillis in two. Heat a little oil in a saucepan and fry the onions till golden brown. Do not allow to burn. Add the potatoes, turmeric, chilli powder and salt to taste and fry well for another 10 minutes. Add the green chillis, sprinkle with a little water, then cover and simmer till potatoes are half-cooked. Add the okra and continue to simmer gently, adding a sprinkling of water if necessary, until cooked. Garnish with the chopped coriander leaves and a little grated or desiccated coconut.

PALAK PANEER

SPINACH AND CREAM CHEESE

Preparation time 15 minutes
Cooking time 45 minutes
To serve 4

You will need

2 lb. spinach
½-inch fresh root ginger
oil for frying
salt to taste
1 teaspoon chilli powder
2 teaspoons ground coriander seeds
1 teaspoon turmeric powder
1 lb. paneer (see page 89)
1 teaspoon garam masala

Wash spinach thoroughly. Mince the ginger very finely. Boil spinach, drain and sieve to purée. Heat some oil in a saucepan. Add the spinach and the rest of the ingredients with the exception of the paneer and garam masala. Cook for 10 minutes. Add the diced, fried paneer to the spinach. Cook for 10 minutes, sprinkle with garam masala and serve.

BHUTTA CURRY

SWEET CORN CURRY

Preparation time 15 minutes
Cooking time 1 hour
To serve 4

You will need

4 corn cobs
oil or butter for frying
1 large onion
2 cloves garlic
1-inch fresh root ginger
½ teaspoon turmeric powder
2-inch stick of cinnamon
3 cloves
3 cardamons
small spring curry leaves *or*
  2 bay leaves
1 teaspoon ground coriander seeds
¼ teaspoon garam masala
1 teaspoon chilli powder
2 cartons yoghurt
salt to taste
pinch of sugar

FOR THE GARNISH

1 chopped green chilli
1 teaspoon chopped coriander leaves

Sweet corn curry

Cut the corn cobs into pieces, mince onion, garlic and ginger very finely together. Fry corn in oil or butter until brown. Remove from the pan and set aside. Now fry the onion, garlic and ginger and when light brown add the turmeric. Cook for one minute and add the rest of the spices and the yoghurt. Cook for about 20 minutes stirring from time to time. Add the corn and salt and cook slowly until the corn is tender. Add the sugar, boil for 1—2 minutes. Serve sprinkled with the green chilli and coriander leaves.

TAMATAR CURRY

TOMATO CURRY

Preparation time 15 minutes
Cooking time 1 hour
To serve 4

You will need

2 lb. tomatoes *or*
28 oz. can peeled tomatoes, drained
1-inch fresh root ginger
3 green chillis
1 large onion
2 cloves garlic
oil for frying
1 rounded teaspoon mustard seeds
sprig of curry leaves *or*
    2 bay leaves
2 tablespoons desiccated coconut, soaked in
    4 tablespoons water
¾ teaspoon chilli powder
1 tablespoon ground coriander
1 teaspoon turmeric powder
salt to taste

Chop half the tomatoes; mince the ginger and green chillis finely, slice the onion and crush the garlic. Heat a little oil in a pan and fry the mustard seeds and curry leaves until the seeds splutter. Add the onion, chopped tomatoes, ginger and chillis. When the onion browns add the strained coconut milk, garlic, chilli powder, coriander, turmeric and salt. Cook gently for 45 minutes. Add the remaining tomatoes 15 minutes before the end of cooking time. Serve with rice.

TAMATAR KA FOOGATH

SPICED TOMATOES

Preparation time 5 minutes
Cooking time 25 minutes
To serve 4

You will need

oil for frying
1 large onion
3 cloves garlic
1½-inch fresh root ginger
3 green chillis
oil for frying
1½ lb. tomatoes, skinned and chopped
1 heaped tablespoon desiccated coconut
salt to taste

Mince or finely chop the onion, garlic, ginger and chillis. Heat a little oil in a pan and fry the onion gently for about five minutes, add the garlic, ginger and chillis and fry for a further 3—4 minutes then add the tomatoes and coconut. Season with salt, mix well and simmer for about 15 minutes.

Tomato curry

PALAK SAG

SPICED SPINACH

Preparation time 10 minutes
Cooking time 30 minutes
To serve 4

You will need

2 lb. spinach
2 large onions
3 green chillis
oil for frying
salt to taste

Wash spinach thoroughly and chop. Slice onions and mince the chillis. Heat some oil in a big pan and fry onions till golden brown. Add chillis and salt, fry for a minute or two and add spinach. Stir, cover and cook for a few minutes. Then uncover and cook so that liquid evaporates.

AVIAL

FRUIT AND VEGETABLE CURRY

Preparation time 15 minutes
Cooking time 25 minutes
To serve 4

You will need

2 bananas, peeled
4 oz. yam
3 sticks celery
1 cucumber
4 oz. courgette
3 tablespoons water
1 teaspoon chilli powder
½ teaspoon turmeric powder
salt to taste
2 green chillis
2 cartons yoghurt (optional)
½ teaspoon ground cummin seeds
2 tablespoons desiccated coconut, soaked in
   2 tablespoons milk
sprig of curry leaves (optional)

Cut the bananas and vegetables into ½-inch thick slices and simmer in a little water with the chilli

Spiced mixed vegetables

powder, turmeric and salt. Meanwhile, mince the green chillis finely and mix with the yoghurt if used, along with the cummin and strained coconut milk. When the vegetables are cooked, drain and return to the cooker. Add the chillis and cook for 5 more minutes. Fry the curry leaves in a little oil and add to the vegetables before serving.

ANANAS CURRY

CURRIED PINEAPPLE

Preparation time 25 minutes
Cooking time 45 minutes
To serve 4

You will need

1 large pineapple (approximately 2 lb.) *or*
   1 × 1 lb. 12 oz. can pineapple, drained
1 large onion
oil for frying
1½ teaspoons chilli powder
1 teaspoon ground coriander seeds
1 tablespoon molasses
salt to taste
½ pint (U.S. 1¼ cups) water

If using fresh pineapple, peel and cut it into small cubes. Slice the onion and fry in a little oil until golden. Add the pineapple, chilli powder and coriander. Cook for five minutes. Add the molasses, salt and water. Simmer for about 30 minutes, until the gravy thickens.

Banana curry

KELA CURRY

BANANA CURRY

Preparation time 5 minutes
Cooking time 25 minutes
To serve 4

You will need

*8 raw green bananas (plantains)
2 green chillis
oil for frying
1 teaspoon mustard seeds
1 teaspoon turmeric powder
salt to taste
1 carton yoghurt
1 teaspoon garam masala

Cut bananas into 1-inch slices, chop the chillis. Heat some oil in a saucepan and fry the mustard seeds and chillis until the mustard seeds pop. Add turmeric, fry for a minute and add the bananas and salt. Fry for a few minutes before adding the yoghurt and garam masala. Cook gently for about 20 minutes.

* This is a special type of banana called *plantain*. It is available in West Indian grocery shops.

Yoghurt with bananas

CURRY ACCOMPANIMENTS

In India we gild the lily. The meal is never complete without papads (paper thin savouries fried or grilled until crisp); a fresh salad of grated carrot; minced tomato and onion; sliced cucumber; green mango seasoned lightly with mustard seed and lime juice; raitha; chutney or pickles.

RAITHA

This is a delightful, easy-to-make salad, using fresh vegetables or fruit combined with yoghurt and seasoning. The favourite combinations are tomato and onion, to which the Southerner adds a mustard seasoning, and the Maharastran in Western India, a sprinkling of chopped peanuts. Banana and guava make a good combination in raitha.

The house-proud Indian wife stocks her larder with pickles and chutneys of her own making. Others who do not have the time or the resources to do so, may buy some of the hundreds of commercially made varieties now available. All Indian and Pa-kistani shops stock a wide range of pickles and chutneys. If you are tempted to try some and have never done so before, I suggest you begin with a mild, sweet mango chutney and later progress to the hotter, more exotic varieties. In India the standard pickles are lime and mango but almost any vegetable — carrot, cauliflower, onion etc. — can be pickled. These are sweet or sour but pungent with chillis, garlic or ginger according to regional liking. In the recipes in this book I have reduced the quantities of garlic and chilli considerably, to suit Western tastes.

Tomatoes, red or green, are especially good for making chutneys and appeal to most tastes. A fresh green chutney made of mint or coriander leaves and chillis, has a pleasant, fresh flavour and is excellent when served with lentils and rice.

Pickles and chutneys are usually served with rice but are also good, especially the sweet variety, with chappatis and puris.

KELA RAITHA

YOGHURT WITH BANANAS

Preparation time   5 minutes
To serve   4

You will need

3 bananas
2 green chillis
salt to taste
1 teaspoon garam masala
coriander leaves
¼ teaspoon chilli powder
3 cartons yoghurt

Slice the bananas and green chillis. Combine with all the other ingredients. Serve with hot puris or as a side dish with curry and rice.

BRINJAL MASALA TARKARI

SPICED AUBERGINES WITH CHILLIS

Preparation time 5 minutes
Cooking time 40 minutes
To serve 4

You will need

1½-2 lb. aubergines
2 green chillis
oil for frying
1 teaspoon mustard seeds
½ teaspoon chilli powder
½ teaspoon ground cummin seeds
½ teaspoon ground coriander seeds
1 carton yoghurt
3 tablespoons water
1 teaspoon sugar
salt to taste

Cut aubergines into halves lengthwise, if very large cut into quarters. Slit chillis into halves. Now heat some oil in a saucepan and fry the mustard seeds. When they begin to crackle add the ground spices and fry for 2—3 minutes. Add the aubergines and fry well. Mix the yoghurt with the water and add to the aubergines along with the green chillis, sugar and salt. Cover and simmer till the aubergines are tender and the gravy thick.

BRINJAL SALAD

AUBERGINE SALAD

Preparation time 10 minutes
Cooking time 40 minutes
To serve 4

You will need

2-3 medium-sized aubergines
2 medium-sized onions
1 green chilli
¼ teaspoon ground black pepper
1 tablespoon vinegar
2 tablespoons salad oil
1 teaspoon sugar
salt to taste

Cut the aubergines in half, lengthways. Bake in a moderate oven (350° F. — Gas Mark 4) for 40 minutes until tender. Scoop out the pulp and put in a bowl. Chop the onion and chilli finely and add to the aubergine along with the other ingredients. Mix well and chill for at least one hour before serving.

BRINJAL ACHAR

AUBERGINE PICKLE

Preparation time 15 minutes
Cooking time 40 minutes

You will need

2 lb. aubergine
salt to taste
4 dry red chillis
1 tablespoon cummin seeds
1½ teaspoon mustard seeds
½ pint (U.S. 1¼ cups) vinegar
6 cloves garlic
3 green chillis
1½-inch fresh root ginger
¼ pint (U.S. 1¼ cups) plus 4 tablespoons salad oil
2 sprigs curry or bay leaves
½ teaspoon turmeric powder
4 oz. sugar

Slice the aubergines, sprinkle with salt, and keep aside. In a mortar, pound together the red chillis, cummin and mustard seeds. Mix with a little vinegar to make a smooth paste. Peel and halve garlic cloves, slit green chillis lengthwise and slice ginger finely. Heat a little of the oil in a pan and fry garlic, chillis and ginger for three minutes. Remove from oil and keep aside. Drain liquid from the aubergines and fry until brown and dry. Drain and remove from the pan. In a clean saucepan fry the curry leaves and spice paste in remaining oil, for three minutes. Add vinegar and when nearly boiling add aubergines, garlic, chillis, ginger and turmeric powder. Cook for two minutes. Add the sugar and salt to taste and cook for 10 minutes. Cool and preserve in air-tight bottles.

Curry accompaniments available from good delicatessen shops

Meat balls in tomato sauce

SALATA

CUCUMBER SALAD

Preparation time 10 minutes
To serve   4-6

You will need

1 cucumber
salt to taste
2 green chillis
juice of 1 lemon *or*
   2 tablespoons vinegar
1 teaspoon sugar

Peel and slice cucumber finely. Put in a bowl and sprinkle with salt and leave for one hour. Discard the liquid, mince chillis, and place cucumber in a dish with chillis. Mix lemon juice, sugar and salt to taste, pour over cucumber, cover and chill before serving.

CACHUMBER

ONION AND TOMATO SALAD

Preparation time 10 minutes
To serve   4-6

You will need

1 large onion
2 large tomatoes
2 green chillis
juice of 1 lemon *or*
   2 tablespoons vinegar
salt to taste

Mince onion. Put tomatoes in a bowl, cover with boiling water for 30 seconds; drain, skin and chop finely. Chop chillis, mix with onion and tomatoes and put in a dish. Add mixed lemon juice and salt. Mix well and chill before serving.

TAMATAR CHUTNEY

TOMATO CHUTNEY (1)

Preparation time 10 minutes
Cooking time   25-30 minutes

You will need

8 oz. tomatoes
1 onion
2 tablespoons vinegar
2 teaspoons chilli powder
salt to taste
1 teaspoon sugar
2 tablespoons oil
$\frac{1}{2}$ teaspoon mustard seeds

Scald, peel and chop the tomatoes finely. Chop the onion and combine with the tomatoes. Place in a bowl with the vinegar, chilli powder, salt and sugar. Heat oil in a pan and fry mustard seeds. As soon as they change colour combine tomato mixture with the remaining ingredients and simmer until chutney thickens. Bottle when cool.

TAMATAR CHUTNEY

TOMATO CHUTNEY (2)

Preparation time 5 minutes
Cooking time   25 minutes

You will need

12 large tomatoes
3 tablespoons vinegar
4 cloves garlic
$\frac{1}{2}$ oz. raisins
$\frac{1}{2}$ oz. salt
$\frac{1}{2}$ oz. sugar
$\frac{1}{2}$ oz. chilli powder
$\frac{1}{4}$ oz. ground mustard seeds

Scald and skin the tomatoes, then parboil them in the vinegar. Crush the garlic and add with all the other ingredients to the tomatoes. Allow it to stand for 12 hours and then boil over a low heat for 20 minutes. When cold, bottle and seal. This chutney will keep for three to four weeks.

TAMATAR DAHI CHUTNEY

TOMATO AND YOGHURT CHUTNEY

Preparation time   15 minutes
Cooking time   5 minutes

You will need

2 large tomatoes
4 green chillis
salt to taste
2 oz. grated *or*
   desiccated coconut
1½ teaspoons mustard seeds
2 cartons yoghurt
1 red chilli
1 tablespoon salad oil

Scald tomatoes in boiling water, peel and cut into small pieces. Using a 'metsaluna', grater or mortar, mince or grind green chillis with the salt and coconut to make a purée. Add ½ teaspoon mustard seeds to the paste, mix well and combine with the tomatoes to the yoghurt. Fry the remaining mustard seeds and red chilli in the oil. When the seeds start to crackle remove from the heat and add to the yoghurt and tomatoes. Mix well and serve when cool. This chutney can be served immediately, it will not keep for long.

MITHI AM CHUTNEY

SWEET MANGO CHUTNEY

Preparation time   20 minutes
Cooking time   50-60 minutes

You will need

2 lbs. half-ripe mangoes
4 tablespoons salt
4 pints (U.S. 10 cups) water
2 oz. fresh root ginger
6 cloves garlic
1 lb. sugar
1 pint (U.S. 2½ cups) vinegar
½ tablespoon chilli powder
½ tablespoon garam masala
4 oz. raisins

Peel and cube mangoes. Make a brine from 4 tablespoons salt and 4 pints (U.S. 10 cups) water and soak mango pieces in it overnight. The next day drain well and dry. Chop ginger and garlic very finely. In a heavy pan dissolve the sugar and vinegar, bring to the boil and simmer for 15 minutes. Add mangoes, ginger and garlic and cook for another 15 minutes, stirring constantly, before adding the remaining spices and raisins. Cook till mixture thickens, remove from heat, cool and bottle in airtight jars.

KHAT MITHI

SOUR SWEET CHUTNEY

Preparation time   30 minutes
Cooking time   45 minutes

You will need

1 lb. green mangoes
8 oz. fresh root ginger
1 oz. almonds
12 dates
¼ oz. peppercorns, freshly ground
2 teaspoons ground cummin seed
½ teaspoon ground cinnamon
1 teaspoon crushed cardamom seeds
6 cloves
1 dessertspoon chilli powder
4 oz. salt
4 oz. raisins
1 pint (U.S. 2½ cups) vinegar
1 lb. sugar

Peel and slice the mangoes, put in a bowl, and set aside. Slice ginger finely, blanch and halve almonds, Slice dates thinly and soak in water for 15 minutes. Put all the dry spices, salt, raisins, almonds and dates in a bowl and mix. Put vinegar and sugar in a saucepan, stir until sugar is dissolved, bring almost to boiling point before adding the spice mixture, mangoes and ginger. Cook and stir till mangoes are tender. Remove from heat, cool and bottle.

AM AUR JINGA KA CHUTNEY

MANGO AND PRAWN CHUTNEY

Preparation time　20 minutes
Cooking time　15 minutes

You will need

4 oz. dried prawns
3 green mangoes
2 onions
1 clove garlic
2 tablespoons salad oil
2 teaspoons chilli powder
2 oz. roasted gram flour
salt to taste

Toast dried prawns in a heavy frying pan and grind or pound to a powder. Peel the mangoes and grate them. Slice the onions and garlic finely. Heat oil and fry the onions and garlic till golden brown. Lower the heat and add prawns, mangoes and remaining ingredients. Mix well and remove from heat. Cool before bottling.

AVAKAI

LEMON PICKLE

Preparation time　15 minutes

You will need

12 lemons
4 oz. salt
2 oz. mustard seeds
½ oz. fenugreek seeds
6 red chillis
6 sliced garlic cloves
1 pint (U.S. 2½ cups) salad oil

Wash lemons and dry thoroughly. Cut in quarters. Pound or crush the dry ingredients with the chillis. Add these with the garlic to the oil. Add the lemon and mix well. Put the mixture into an air-tight bottle or jar and shake every three days. The pickle will be ready to eat after 4 weeks.

KOTHMIR PUDINA KI CHUTNEY (1)

FRESH HERB CHUTNEY

Preparation time　10 minutes
Cooking time　15 minutes
To serve　4

You will need

2 oz. fresh coriander *or*
　mint leaves
2 green chillis
2 potatoes
juice of 1 lemon
salt to taste

Mince leaves finely with the green chillis. Peel, boil and mash the potatoes and add to the coriander and chillis along with the lemon juice and salt to taste. Alternatively, put all the ingredients in a blender.

KOTHMIR PUDINA KI CHUTNEY (2)

FRESH HERB CHUTNEY

Preparation time　15 minutes
To serve　4

You will need

2 oz. fresh coriander *or*
　mint leaves
2 green chillis
* 1 oz. tamarind, soaked in
　4 tablespoons boiling water
1 teaspoon sugar
salt to taste

* Squeeze the tamarind, discard the husk and use only the water.

Mince leaves finely with the green chillis. Soak the tamarind in boiling water for 30 minutes. Mix the tamarind liquid with minced leaves and chillis, add the remaining ingredients and mix thoroughly.

HAR MIRCH ACHAR

GREEN CHILLI PICKLE

Preparation time   15 minutes
Cooking time   15 minutes

You will need

4 oz. fresh root ginger
1 oz. garlic
1 oz. cummin seeds
1 oz. mustard seeds
½ pint (U.S. 1¼ cups) salad oil
* 4 oz. tamarind, soaked in
    ¼ pint (U.S. ⅔ cup) boiling water
4 oz. brown sugar
½ pint (U.S. 1¼ cups) malt vinegar
8 oz. small green chillis

* Squeeze the tamarind, discard the husk, use only the water.

Finely mince or grate the ginger and garlic, pound the cummin and mustard seeds and mix with a little vinegar to make a paste. Heat the oil in a pan and fry the paste well. Then add the strained tamarind juice, brown sugar and vinegar. Bring to the boil and add the green chillis. Lower heat and simmer for 10 minutes. Bottle when cold.

JINGA ACHAR

PRAWN PICKLE

Preparation time   20 minutes
Cooking time   20-25 minutes

You will need

2 pints prawns, shelled and de-veined
1 teaspoon chilli powder
1 teaspoon turmeric powder
salt to taste
¼ pint (U.S. ⅔ cup) salad oil
1 teaspoon cummin seeds
1 teaspoon mustard seeds
1 teaspoon fenugreek seeds
1 teaspoon curry powder
5 cloves garlic
½ pint (U.S. 1¼ cups) vinegar

Savoury yoghurt

Roll the prawns in a little masala — made by mixing the chilli powder, salt and turmeric with a little vinegar. Heat some oil in a frying pan and fry the prawns well. Roast the cummin, mustard and fenugreek seeds in an iron frying pan and then pound in a mortar to a fine powder. Place the powdered seeds in a deep saucepan on the stove, pour in the oil and, when it is warm, add the curry powder and garlic. Add prawns, vinegar and salt. Bring to the boil and then lower heat and simmer gently for a few minutes. Cool and bottle in an air-tight jar.

SUDEVAW

SAVOURY YOGHURT

Preparation time   10 minutes
To serve   4

You will need

2 green chillis
2 tablespoons desiccated coconut, soaked in
    2 tablespoons hot water
* 1 walnut-sized piece tamarind,
    soaked in 2 tablespoons boiling water
4 cartons yoghurt
salt to taste
½ teaspoon sugar
1 tablespoon chopped coriander leaves
1 small packet potato crisps

* Squeeze and strain. Discard the husk, use only the liquid.

Mince or chop the chillis as finely as possible. Combine with the remaining ingredients.

JEERA PANI

CUMMIN SEED DRINK

Preparation time　15 minutes
To serve　　　　　4

You will need

½ oz. fresh mint
½ oz. fresh root ginger
1 dessertspoon ground white cummin seeds
½ teaspoon chilli powder
½ teaspoon garam masala
2 teaspoons salt
2 teaspoons sugar
2 tablespoons lemon juice
1½ pints (U.S. 3¾ cups) water
* 2 oz. tamarind, soaked in
　¾ pint (U.S. 2 cups) water overnight

FOR THE GARNISH

Slices of lemon and mint leaves

---

* Squeeze the tamarind and discard the husk. Strain the liquid before use.

Chop mint and ginger. Mix with all the other ingredients. Add to the tamarind water and mix well. Taste and adjust the seasoning. Refrigerate for 2—3 hours and serve in small glasses without stirring.

DAHI BUNDI

YOGHURT WITH BATTER FRITTERS

Preparation time　10 minutes
Cooking time　　　15 minutes
To serve　　　　　4

You will need

4 oz. gram flour
salt to taste
pinch bicarbonate of soda
water to mix
oil for frying
3 cartons yoghurt
2 green chillis
freshly ground black pepper
1 teaspoon cummin seeds
½ teaspoon mustard seeds
1 sprig curry leaves *or*
　2 bay leaves

FOR THE GARNISH

1 tablespoon coriander leaves

Sieve flour, salt and bicarbonate of soda into a bowl. Whisk in sufficient water to make a medium batter. Heat some oil in a deep frying pan and fry the batter by letting it drop through the holes of a perforated spoon into the oil. Fry until golden brown and drain. Put the yoghurt into a serving bowl add the the fried batter balls, finely minced chillis, pepper, cummin seeds and salt. Fry the mustard seeds and curry leaves, add to the yoghurt and mix well. Garnish with chopped coriander leaves.

Gram flour biscuits

SNACKS

For its range of snacks and teatime savouries, Indian cooking is hard to beat. Tea drinking may be an imported habit but the serving of a snack is a very Indian custom, known all over the country.

Pakoras — a kind of fritter, the commonest snack made in India — is quick and simple to make. It can be made from any available vegetable and a batter made from gram flour and water.

There are some refreshing appetisers containing specially chosen spices that are served just before or during a meal to promote the appetite and as an aid to digestion. Rasam from the South, ranges from a fiery pepper-water to a mild tomato flavoured drink. Jeera Pani, made from cummin seeds, is especially good for toning down a heavy meal.

Snacks are almost always vegetarian although 'samosas', pastry envelopes with a filling, are also made with minced meat. Many of these snacks are served with a chutney or a savoury sauce. Try some of these with drinks or perhaps as a quick 'elevenses', or with afternoon tea.

SEV GATIA

GRAM FLOUR BISCUIT

Preparation time   15 minutes
Cooking time   20-30 minutes
To serve   4

You will need

1 tablespoon ghee or oil
8 oz. gram flour
1 teaspoon caraway seeds
½ teaspoon turmeric powder
pinch of chilli powder
salt to taste
2-4 tablespoons water
oil or ghee for deep frying

Warm the ghee slightly and pour into the sieved flour. Add caraway, turmeric, chilli, salt and water and mix to a stiff dough. Heat oil or ghee for deep frying. Put dough into vermicelli machine or Mouli shredder, hold the machine six inches above the hot ghee and pass the dough through to form strips. Fry till crisp and golden. Sev may be preserved in an air-tight tin and make a delicious tea time snack.

MATTHIES

FRIED SAVOURY BISCUITS

Preparation time 35 minutes
Cooking time 3-5 minutes
To serve 4-6

You will need

8 oz. plain flour
salt to taste
2½ oz. butter
1 dessertspoon cummin *or*
  caraway seeds
3 tablespoons milk
hot water to mix
oil for deep frying

Sieve the flour and salt into a mixing bowl. Heat the butter in a small pan until it bubbles. Pour it into the flour and add the cummin or caraway seeds. Stir well and add the milk and sufficient hot water to make a firm dough. Turn out on to a board and knead for 20 minutes. Roll out thinly and cut into strips, triangles or squares.
Heat oil in a deep frying pan. Fry until crisp and golden. Drain and serve.

VARIATION:

2 teaspoons of coarsley ground pepper may be added to the dough, to make spiced matthies.

RICE VADAM

FRIED RICE BALLS

Preparation time 10 minutes
Cooking time 10 minutes
To serve 4

You will need

4 oz. rice, cooked and drained
3 teaspoons chilli powder
salt to taste
½ teaspoon asafoetida (optional)
oil or ghee for frying

Pound the cooked rice, chilli powder, salt and asafoetida to a paste in a mortar or grind in a liquidiser. Roll the paste into little balls. Arrange them on a clean tea cloth and put them in a warm place to dry. When completely dry they can be stored in an air-tight tin. When required, deep fry in ghee or oil until crisp. Drain and serve hot.

ANDHRA-UPUMA

SAVOURY SEMOLINA

Preparation time 10 minutes
Cooking time 30 minutes
To serve 4

You will need

8 oz. semolina
2 large onions
2 green chillis
2 oz. cashew nuts
1 oz. butter
3 tablespoons oil
1 teaspoon mustard seeds
1½ teaspoons black gram dhal
1 tablespoon chopped coriander leaves
½ pint (U.S. 1¼ cups) water
½ teaspoon ground cinnamon
½ teaspoon ground cloves
juice of 2 lemons
salt to taste

Put the semolina on a baking sheet and brown it in a hot oven. Set aside when ready. Meanwhile, chop the onions, chillis and cashew nuts. Heat the butter and oil in a saucepan. Add the mustard seeds and fry until they crackle. Put the dhal and cashew nuts into the pan and fry for a minute. Add the onions and coriander leaves. Cook for five minutes. Add half the water together with the remaining ingredients, except the semolina. Stir and cook for one minute then add the remaining water and cook for a further 15 minutes, stirring occasionally. Gradually sprinkle in the semolina and cook for five minutes stirring constantly. Add more water if mixture is too dry. The result will be a thick paste. Cover the saucepan with a tight-fitting lid and cook gently until the mixture dries out. Remove lid and allow the steam to evaporate. Serve piping hot with coffee.

Egg and minced lamb

Lamb with spiced onions

KELE-KA-PURIS

BANANA PANCAKES

Preparation time   5 minutes
Cooking time   15 minutes
To serve   4

You will need

2 oz. gram flour
4 oz. plain flour
salt to taste
½ teaspoon chilli powder
½ teaspoon ground cummin seeds
pinch of turmeric powder
1 tablespoon ghee or oil
2 bananas
2 green chillis
½ teaspoon sugar

Combine the gram and plain flour in a bowl. Add salt, chilli powder, ground cummin, turmeric and the ghee or oil and mix until well blended. Mash the bananas and mix with finely minced green chillis and sugar. Add to the flour and knead to a smooth dough, adding a little water if necessary. Divide the dough into 16 portions and roll into wafer-thin circles. Cook on a greased griddle or in an iron frying pan, turning once, to brown both sides.

SOJI PAKORI

SEMOLINA FRITTERS

Preparation time   25 minutes
Cooking time   5 minutes
To serve   4

You will need

8 oz. semolina
8 tablespoons water
1 carton yoghurt
2 oz. peas, cooked
oil for frying
2 green chillis
pinch of asafoetida (optional)
2 onions, chopped
salt to taste
1 tablespoon chopped coriander leaves

Sieve semolina into a bowl. Add water and yoghurt. Set aside for about 15—20 minutes. Add the peas to the semolina. Fry the chopped chillis and asafoetida, if used, in a little oil and add to the semolina with the chopped onions, salt and coriander leaves. Mould the mixture into little balls and deep fry until brown. Serve hot with chutney or pickle.

KODU BALE

SAVOURY RICE FLOUR FRITTERS

Preparation time   10 minutes
Cooking time   10 minutes
To serve   4

You will need

8 oz. rice flour
2 tablespoons ghee or oil
2 tablespoons desiccated coconut, soaked in
   3 tablespoons milk
½ teaspoon chilli powder
1 teaspoon cummin seeds
salt to taste
oil for deep frying

Put the rice flour in a bowl. Heat the ghee or oil and pour into the rice flour. Squeeze and discard the coconut. Strain the milk and add to the flour with the rest of the ingredients. Knead into a soft dough, adding water if necessary. Form the dough into thin cigar shapes and deep fry until golden. Drain and serve immediately.

Savoury rice flour fritters

MOONG PAKORA

BAMBOO SHOOT FRITTERS (1)

Preparation time   15 minutes
Cooking time   15 minutes
To serve   4

You will need

1 bamboo shoot
4 oz. gram flour
¼ pint (U.S. ⅔ cup) water
½ teaspoon chilli powder
salt to taste
oil for deep frying

Clean, wash and slice the bamboo shoot finely. Sieve gram flour into a bowl and mix with the water to make a thickish batter. Add chilli powder and salt. Mix well and add the bamboo shoot. Heat oil in a deep frying pan and drop teaspoonsful of the batter into the hot oil. Fry until golden. Drain and serve hot.

MOONG PAKORA

BEAN SPROUT FRITTERS (2)

Preparation time   15 minutes
Cooking time   15 minutes
To serve   4

You will need

8 oz. fresh *or*
  canned bean sprouts
2 onions
2 green chillis
1 tablespoon chopped coriander leaves
½ teaspoon chilli powder
2 oz. plain flour
salt to taste
pinch of bicarbonate of soda
1 egg
milk to mix

Place bean sprouts in a pan with sufficient water to cover. Simmer until tender, drain and put in a bowl. (If using canned bean sprouts just drain.) Chop onions and chillis and add them to the bean sprouts along with the coriander leaves, chilli powder, flour, salt, and bicarbonate of soda. Mix thoroughly. Beat in the egg and a little milk to form a thick batter. Heat a greased griddle or frying pan. Drop teaspoonsful of the mixture into the pan. Cook until golden on both sides, turning once.

BATATA VADA

SPICED POTATO FRITTERS

Preparation time   10 minutes
Cooking time   35 minutes
To serve   4

You will need

2 green chillis
1-inch fresh root ginger
2 teaspoons fresh coriander leaves
1 lb. potatoes, mashed
1 tablespoon desiccated coconut, soaked in
1 tablespoon warm milk
1 teaspoon turmeric powder
salt to taste
2 teaspoons lemon juice
2 oz. rice flour
2 oz. gram flour
water to mix
oil for deep frying

Finely mince chillis, ginger and coriander leaves and add to potatoes with coconut, turmeric, salt and lemon juice. Mix well, shape into balls then flatten to make small patties. Mix rice and gram flours together with a little salt and add water to make a thin batter. Dip potato patties in batter and fry in oil till crisp and golden.

PAKORAS

SAVOURY FRITTERS

Preparation time   10 minutes
Cooking time   5 minutes
To serve   4

You will need

8 oz. gram flour
½ teaspoon chilli powder
1 teaspoon turmeric powder
½ teaspoon ground coriander seeds
salt to taste
¼ teaspoon baking powder
water to mix
4 oz. potatoes
1 aubergine
few spinach, cabbage or spring green leaves
oil for deep frying

Sieve the flour, chilli powder, turmeric, coriander, salt and baking powder into a mixing bowl. Add sufficient water to make a thick batter. Cut the vegetables into thin slices, dip them in the batter and deep fry in hot oil until crisp.

ONION PAKORAS

ONION FRITTERS

Preparation time   15 minutes
Cooking time   15 minutes
To serve   4

You will need

4 oz. gram flour
2 teaspoons chilli powder
salt to taste
water to mix
4 onions
oil or ghee for frying

Onion fritters

Sieve the flour, chilli powder and salt into a bowl. Beat in sufficient water to make a thin batter. Cut onions into rings ⅛-inch thick. Heat oil or ghee in a frying pan. Dip onion rings into the batter. Fry quickly until crisp. Drain and serve with hot tomato chutney.

MITHI PAKORI

COCONUT AND BANANA FRITTERS

Preparation time   15 minutes
Cooking time   15 minutes
To serve   4

You will need

4 oz. plain flour
½ teaspoon baking powder
½ teaspoon vanilla essence
2 tablespoons desiccated coconut, soaked in
  a little milk
2 large bananas
1 egg, whisked with
  1 tablespoon sugar
ghee or oil for frying

Sieve flour and baking powder into a mixing bowl. Add vanilla essence, strained coconut milk and mashed bananas. Mix well. Beat in the whisked egg and sugar. If necessary add water to make a smooth, medium-thick batter. Heat a little ghee or oil in a pan and drop in spoonsful of batter. Cook the fritters till golden on both sides. Serve immediately.

KACHORIS

STUFFED FRIED PASTRY PUFFS

Preparation time   20 minutes
Cooking time   30 minutes
To serve   4

You will need

1½ oz. each almonds, pistachios, walnuts and
   cashewnuts
12 oz. peas, shelled
water
1 dessertspoon coriander leaves
2 green chillis
1½ oz. sultanas
juice of ½ lemon
1 teaspoon garam masala
1 tablespoon desiccated coconut

FOR THE PASTRY

12 oz. plain flour
pinch of bicarbonate of soda
pinch of salt
1 tablespoon melted butter
water to mix
oil for deep frying

Blanch the nuts if necessary. Put in a saucepan with
the peas and a little water and simmer for at least

Minced meat pasties

10 minutes. Drain and pass through a mincer or
'Mouli' grater. Finely chop the coriander leaves and
green chillis and add to the purée along with the
sultanas, lemon juice, garam masala and coconut.
Sieve the flour, bicarbonate of soda and salt into a
bowl. Add the butter and enough cold water to
mix to a dough. Divide dough into 16 portions and
roll into round, very thin pancakes. Place a spoonful of the purée in the centre of each. Gather the
edges of the pancakes together and pinch to seal. Pat
or roll into squares and deep fry until golden. Serve
with chutney or tomato sauce.

KHEEMA SAMOSA

MINCED MEAT PASTIES

Preparation time   30 minutes
Cooking time   1 hour
To serve   4

You will need

FOR THE PASTRY

4 oz. plain flour
pinch salt
1 oz. butter
2 tablespoons warm milk

FOR THE STUFFING

1 onion
1 tomato
1 green chilli
1 tablespoon coriander leaves
1 clove garlic
oil for frying
8 oz. lean minced lamb or beef
½ teaspoon chilli powder
½ teaspoon turmeric powder
½ teaspoon garam masala
salt to taste
2 teaspoons lemon juice

Sieve flour with salt. Rub in butter till it resembles
breadcrumbs. Add milk and knead to a stiff, smooth
dough. Cover and set aside. Finely chop onion,
tomato, chilli and coriander leaves. Crush the
garlic. Heat some oil in a pan and fry the onion and
garlic for about 10 minutes. Add the green chilli
and fry for two minutes. Stir in the meat and fry
well till the meat turns brown. Add tomato, coriander leaves, chilli powder, turmeric and garam ma-

sala. Season with salt and simmer very gently, adding a little water if necessary, for 20 minutes or till meat is tender, and all liquid absorbed. Sprinkle with lemon juice, mix and keep aside to cool.

Divide the pastry into 6 equal pieces. Roll each into a thin circular shape, dust with flour to make rolling easier. Cut each circle in half and place a spoonful of meat on each semi-circle. Fold the pastry over, moisten the edges with water and seal carefully fo form triangularshaped pasties. Heat some oil for deep frying and fry the samosas on both sides till golden brown. Drain and serve hot with chutney or yoghurt.

SABZI SAMOSA

VEGETABLE PASTIES

Preparation time   30 minutes
Cooking time   30 minutes
To serve   4

You will need

FOR THE PASTRY

4 oz. plain flour
pinch of salt
1 oz. butter
2 tablespoons warm milk

FOR THE STUFFING

1 onion
2 green chillis
½-inch fresh root ginger
1 teaspoon fresh coriander leaves
oil for frying
½ teaspoon mustard seeds
½ teaspoon turmeric powder
4 oz. peas, shelled
½ teaspoon garam masala
salt to taste
4 oz. potatoes, boiled and cubed
2 teaspoons lemon juice

Make the pastry as described in the previous recipe. Finely mince onion, chillis, ginger and coriander leaves, separately. Heat some oil in a pan and fry mustard seeds. When they begin to crackle add onion and fry till golden. Add chillis, ginger, and turmeric, fry for two minutes and add peas, garam masala and salt. Cook till peas are done. Add potatoes, coriander leaves and lemon juice, mix well and

cook for one more minute. Remove from heat and cool. Fill and cook the samosas as described in recipe above.

SINGARA

SPICED VEGETABLE PUFFS

Preparation time   20 minutes
Cooking time   45 minutes
To serve   4

You will need

1 large potato
1 small onion
1 tomato
½-inch fresh root ginger
oil for frying
1 teaspoon garam masala
1 teaspoon chilli powder
½ teaspoon sugar
3 oz. peas, shelled
1 tablespoon rasins blanched
2 teaspoons chopped coriander leaves
1 tablespoon lemon juice
salt to taste

FOR THE PASTRY

8 oz. plain flour
pinch of baking powder
1 tablespoon melted butter
2-3 tablespoons warm milk
oil for deep frying

Boil the potato in its jacket. Dice finely and set aside. Chop onion and tomato, finely mince the ginger. Fry onion in a little oil till golden, add tomato and ginger and fry for 1—2 minutes. Add the garam masala, chilli powder, sugar, peas and cook till peas are tender. Add water if necessary. Stir in the chopped potato and fry for five minutes. Remove from the heat and mix in the raisins, coriander leaves, lemon juice and salt. For the pastry, sieve the flour, salt and baking powder into a bowl and mix to a firm dough with the butter, milk and a little water if necessary. Knead well and roll out thinly into circles. Cut each in half put a spoonful of the stuffing on each, damp the edges of the pastry and fold to form a triangle. Seal edges well and deep fry in oil till golden. Serve hot.

BHAJI PURIS

STUFFED PURI WITH CHILLI SAUCE

Preparation time   30 minutes
Cooking time   45 minutes
To serve   4

You will need

FOR THE PURIS

8 oz. whole meal or plain flour
1 teaspoon salt
¼ teaspoon ground coriander
¼ teaspoon turmeric powder
¼ teaspoon chilli powder
water to mix

FOR THE FILLING

4 oz. cauliflower, cooked
1 tablespoon dessicated coconut, soaked in
  1 tablespoon hot water
1 oz. peanuts
2 green chillis
1 teaspoon chopped coriander leaves
juice of ½ lemon
½ teaspoon sugar
salt to taste

oil for frying

FOR THE SAUCE

2 green chillis
* 1 oz. tamarind, soaked in
  6 tablespoons boiling water
1 tablespoon molasses
½ teaspoon mustard seeds
oil for frying
pinch of salt

* When the tamarind is soft squeeze and discard the husk. Strain the liquid before use.

Make the puris by sieving the dry ingredients into a mixing bowl. Then add sufficient water to make a firm dough. Knead well till dough is smooth. Divide into 16 equal portions. Shape each portion into a ball, flatten and roll, on a well-floured board, into thin pancakes. For the filling put the cauliflour in a bowl, mash, chop coriander leaves finely and add to cauliflour with remaining ingredients. Mix well and put equal quantities in the centre of half the puris, dampen the edges and place the remaining puris on top. Press down edges, and seal. Put tamarind water, chillis and molasses into a small pan and simmer gently for 20 minutes. Fry the mustard seeds in a little oil. When they turn white add them to the ingredients in the pan. Cover and bring to the boil then remove from heat. Deep fry the puris in hot oil. Drain and serve with the Chilli Sauce.

Paratha stuffed with potatoes

AKOORI

SPICED SCRAMBLED EGG

Preparation time   10 minutes
Cooking time   15 minutes
To serve   4

You will need

butter for frying
1 large onion, sliced finely
2 tomatoes, skinned and chopped
3 green chillis, chopped
1 tablespoon chopped coriander leaves
½ teaspoon turmeric powder
salt to taste
8 eggs
4 slices hot buttered toast

Melt some butter in a pan and gently fry the onions till golden. Add the tomatoes, chillis, coriander leaves, turmeric and salt and fry till tomatoes are cooked. Add the beaten eggs and cook on a low heat till eggs are scrambled. Serve on the toast.

MASALA TOAST

SAVOURY TOAST

Preparation time   5 minutes
Cooking time   5 minutes
To serve   4

Masala toast

You will need

2 large slices bread, ½-inch thick
4 tablespoons milk
2 eggs
pepper and salt to taste
1 small clove garlic, crushed
¼ teaspoon ground ginger
1 dessertspoon chopped fresh mint

Remove crusts from the bread and soak the bread in the milk. Beat the eggs with the remaining ingredients and pour over the bread. Shallow fry till brown on both sides. Serve a half round to each person with sliced tomatoes.

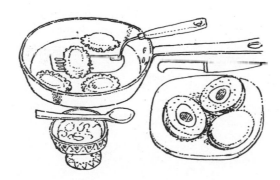

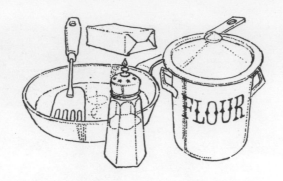

BREAD

Bread (roti) in India usually means unleavened bread. Made of wholemeal wheat flour, the *chappati* is the staple food of the North. It is as tasty to eat as it is simple to make. The flat, pancake-shaped chappati is the simplest form of bread — just flour, salt and water and a little fat to grease the griddle. The *phulka*, a grander version of the chappati, is thinner and when cooked is placed in the cinders or on a low open flame until it puffs up. *Parathas* are a fried layered bread made by folding and rolling the dough a number of times while *puris* are made of the same ingredients but rolled thinly to a small saucer-size and then fried till they are puffed up and golden brown.

Nan is a leavened bread made with flour, egg, yoghurt, yeast and butter. It is usually grilled in a tandoor but can be partly cooked in an ordinary oven and partly under a grill. A word about *papads* or *papadams*. I have not given a recipe for them; the preparation is very laborious when it is considered that they can be bought in almost any delicatessen shop and most good supermarkets. Simply deep fry or grill before serving.

For success in making the softest, thinnest *rotis*, the following rules must be observed:

a) The dough must be thoroughly kneaded for at least 25 minutes.

b) The amount of water used to make the dough must be adjusted to suit the quality of flour used — certain types of flour absorb more water than others.

c) A heavy griddle or frying pan is essential. In India a shallow, curved griddle called a 'tawa' is used. A tawa could be used on a gas cooker but not on an electric one.

Almost all the breads, for which various recipes follow, must be eaten immediately after preparation, as they tend to become soggy and limp upon keeping.

PURIS

DEEP FRIED BREAD

(Ilustrated in colour on opposite page)

Preparation time   20 minutes
Cooking time   30 minutes
To serve   4

You will need

4 oz. wholemeal flour
4 oz. plain flour
1 teaspoon salt
2 teaspoons melted butter

¼ pint (U.S. ⅔ cup) warm water
oil for deep frying

Mix the flour and salt. Make a depression in the centre and add the butter. Knead to a stiff dough by gradually adding water. Knead for 10—15 minutes till the dough is soft and pliable. Cover and set aside for 15 minutes. Now divide the dough into 16 equal portions and roll into thin round pancakes. Heat some oil in a frying pan and fry the puris quickly, turning during cooking. Press sides of the puris with a fish slice whilst frying and splash the tops with hot oil to encourage them to puff up. Drain when golden brown on both sides.

Fried bread

Spiced lamb chops

MATAR PARATHA

STUFFED WHOLEMEAL BREAD

Preparation time 40 minutes
Cooking time 30 minutes
To serve 4

You will need

1 tablespoon desiccated coconut
2 green chillis
salt to taste
½ teaspoon ground cloves
1 teaspoon ground coriander seeds
¼ teaspoon ground cummin seeds
½ clove garlic
½-inch fresh root ginger
1 tablespoon chopped coriander leaves
2 springs mint
8 oz. peas, cooked
juice of ½ lemon

FOR THE DOUGH

4 oz. wholemeal flour
4 oz. plain flour
salt to taste
1 tablespoon melted butter
8 tablespoons water
butter for greasing

Mix the coconut, chillis, salt and spices with the garlic, ginger, coriander and mint. Mince or pound to make a coarse paste. Add the peas with the lemon juice and mash together. Divide the mixture into six balls, and set aside. Combine both types of flour and the salt. Mix in the melted butter and gradually add the water. Knead sufficiently to make a soft, smooth dough. Cover and set aside for 10 minutes. Divide into twelve equal parts. Roll out into thin pancakes and place a portion of filling in the centre of six of them. Spread the filling over the surface leaving ½ inch all round. Damp the edges with a little water. Cover with the remaining pastry circles and seal the edges. Heat a heavy frying pan or griddle and grease with a little butter. Fry each paratha until golden brown on both sides, greasing with additional butter if necessary. Serve immediately.

PARATHA

INDIAN FRIED BREAD

Preparation time 30 minutes
Cooking time 5 minutes
To serve 4

You will need

6 oz. whole wheat flour
6 oz. white flour
2 tablespoons melted butter
¼ pint (U.S. ⅔ cup) plus 2 tablespoons water
pinch of salt

Mix both types of flour together on to a pastry board or into a mixing bowl. Mix in one tablespoon of melted butter and the salt. Gradually add enough water and knead sufficiently to make a soft dough. Cover and set aside for 10 minutes. Divide the dough into eight portions. Roll each portion into a ball, flatten between the palms of your hands and roll out into a thin circle on the board. Brush with a little melted butter and fold over into a semi-circle. Brush again lightly with butter and fold into a quarter circle. Now roll out into a triangular shape ⅛-inch thick. Grease a hot griddle or frying pan and place the paratha on it. Cook on one side for a minute, turn over and brush with butter. Brush around the edges with butter and cook till golden brown.

Paratha

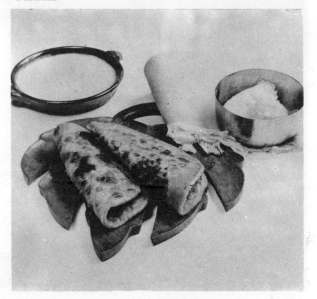

CHAPPATI

INDIAN BREAD

Preparation time 30 minutes
Cooking time 5 minutes
To serve 4

You will need

8 oz. whole wheat flour
pinch of salt
¼ pint (U.S. ⅔ cup) plus 2 tablespoons water
melted butter

Sieve flour and salt onto a pastry board or a large plate. Make a hole in the centre of the flour and add 8 tablespoons of the water. Knead well for 15 minutes to form a soft dough. Add the rest of the water gradually, kneading another 10 minutes. Leave to stand for 30 minutes. Divide into 10—12 portions and roll out into thin round pancakes. Meanwhile heat a griddle or heavy frying pan then cook one chappati at a time. Press to flatten when small blisters appear on the surface then turn and cook on the other side till lightly golden. Brush a little butter on one side and serve.

NAN

BAKED LEAVENED BREAD

Preparation time 45 minutes
Cooking time 15-20 minutes
To serve 4

You will need

8 oz. flour
1 teaspoon sugar
½ teaspoon baking powder
½ teaspoon salt
scant ¼ pint (U.S. ¾ cup) milk
1 carton yoghurt
1 oz. yeast dissolved in
  a little of the milk
1 oz. melted butter *or*
  1 egg yolk
1 tablespoon poppy seeds

Sift the flour, sugar, baking powder and salt. Warm the milk and yoghurt, and add the yeast, butter and egg. Mix to combine thoroughly. Make a depression in the centre of the flour and pour in the mixture a little at a time until all is absorbed. Knead well for 15 minutes till smooth and springy, adding a little more flour if the dough is sticky. Cover and

Chappati

Nan

ALU KI ROTI

PARATHA STUFFED WITH POTATO

Preparation time   35 minutes
Cooking time   1 hour
To serve   4

You will need

8 oz. potatoes
1 onion
2 green chillis
1 clove garlic
1 oz. butter
½ teaspoon garam masala
¼ teaspoon ground ginger
1 teaspoon ground cummin seeds
½ teaspoon chilli powder
¼ teaspoon turmeric powder
¼ teaspoon pepper
salt to taste
1 tablespoon finely chopped coriander leaves
paratha dough (see page 135)

leave to rise until double in bulk (approximately three — four hours, unless the weather is hot, in which case the dough might rise in half the time). Divide into eight portions and roll into balls with well floured hands. Cover and set aside for another 15 minutes. Flatten each ball into a thick pancake with the help of a little flour by tossing from one palm of the hand to the other. Brush tops with melted butter or egg yolk and sprinkle with poppy seeds. Bake in a very hot oven (450° F. — Gas Mark 8) for about 10 minutes. The nan should puff up and brown. An alternative method is to cook on a hot griddle and when one side is done, place raw side up under a grill.

Boil the potatoes in their skins, then peel and dice into small cubes. Chop the onion and chillis finely, then crush the garlic and fry in butter with the spices, seasoning and potatoes. Fry well till dry. Mash the mixture with a fork and when cool divide into six equal portions. Divide the paratha dough into six portions, roll each portion into a ball and flatten it in the palm of the hand. Put a portion of the potato mixture in the centre, fold the dough over to cover and re-shape into a ball. Roll out on a pastry board as thinly as possible. Cook as for paratha.

Carrot sweet

DESSERTS AND SWEETS

Although it is not customary to end a meal with a dessert a sweet dish is often served as part of the meal. 'Sweeten the mouth of your guest' is an Indian maxim — visitors are welcomed with sweets. At marriage feasts in Southern India the sweet is served first, as a happy augury.

Most Indian sweets are made of milk and sugar with variations in flavourings like coconut, almonds, pistachios, cardamoms, rose water, kewra (essence of flower of the kewra plant) or saffron. There are roughly two different types of milk sweets. The one made from *khoa* or *mawa*, a milk preparation made by boiling milk until it becomes solid. The other is made from *paneer* or *chenna*, a cream cheese.

Khoa is made by briskly boiling 1 pint of Jersey milk in a heavy pan. Constant stirring is required to prevent the milk from catching. After 25—30 minutes the milk reduces to a thick lump. It is removed from the heat at this stage. A pint of Jersey milk yields about 3 oz. khoa (a less rich milk can be used but the yield will be less).

A recipe for *paneer* or *chenna*, as it is sometimes called, is given on page 89.

Besides the milk sweets there are a number of sweets made of gram flour, cornflour and semolina. In India, ghee (clarified butter) is always used in sweet making. In the following recipes I have replaced it entirely, with unsalted butter.

GAJJAR KA HALWA

CARROT SWEET

Preparation time   10 minutes
Cooking time   1 hour 20 minutes
To serve   4

You will need

8 oz. carrots
1½ pints (U.S. 3¾ cups) milk
5 oz. sugar
1 dessertspoon golden syrup
2½ oz. unsalted butter
1 oz. sultanas

FOR DECORATION

6 cardamom seeds crushed
few blanched almonds

Prepare the carrots if necessary, then grate them and put into a heavy pan with the milk. Cook the mixture steadily, stirring frequently with a spoon until it becomes almost solid (this can take up to an hour). Now add the sugar, the golden syrup, butter and sultanas and cook, taking care to stir continuously, until the mixture starts to leave the sides of the pan. This will take approximately 15—20 minutes.

Grease a shallow tin and spread the mixture into it evenly. Sprinkle with the crushed cardamom seeds and decorate with a few blanched almonds, if desired.

RASGULLA

CREAM CHEESE SWEET

Preparation time 40 minutes
Cooking time 1 hour
To serve 4

You will need

FOR THE CREAM CHEESE BALLS

paneer, made from 2 pints (U.S. 5 cups) milk
  (see page 89)
1 teaspoon plain flour
pinch of bicarbonate of soda

FOR THE SYRUP

2 lb sugar
2 pints (U.S. 5 cups) water
1 teaspoon of rose water *or*
  few drops of kewra essence

After making the paneer put it in a large bowl or on a plate and knead with the palm of the hand until it becomes smooth and soft. Add the flour and bicarbonate of soda and knead for a few more minutes. Roll and shape the mixture into small balls. Dissolve the sugar in the water over gentle heat. Boil to 220° F. or soft ball. Divide the syrup in to two parts. Leave one aside and bring the other to boiling point and gently slip in the cream cheese balls. Simmer for 10 minutes then cook slightly

Cauliflower sweet

faster adding a little water to thin the syrup. When the cheese balls (rasgu llas) float under the surface they are ready. Drain and put them in the remaining syrup. Sprinkle with rose water, allow to stand for a few hours before serving.

DOODH BARE

BATTER BALL PUDDING

Preparation time 25 minutes
Cooking time 1¼ hours
To serve 4

You will need

4 oz. plain flour
1 tablespoon melted butter
water to mix
cloves
oil for deep frying
2 pints (U.S. 5 cups) milk
4 oz. sugar
2 oz. raisins, soaked in water
2 oz. almonds
1 tablespoon coconut
2 oz. each pistachio and hazlenuts
10 cardamom seeds, crushed

Sieve flour into a bowl. Add melted butter and sufficient water to make a soft dough. Divide and shape the dough into walnut-sized balls. Stick a clove in each ball. Heat the oil and deep fry each ball until the underside puffs up. Turn over and cook on the other side. Drain when golden brown. Boil the milk in a large pan until half the milk has evaporated (about 30 minutes). Add the sugar and cool. Add the puffs, strained raisins, and remaining ingredients. Serve when puffs are quite soft.

GULAB JAMUNS

MILK SWEETS IN SYRUP

Preparation time 1½ hours
Cooking time 30 minutes
To serve 4

You will need

FOR THE SYRUP

1½ lb. sugar
2 pints (U.S. 5 cups) water
1 teaspoon rose water

FOR THE SWEETS

3 oz. khoa, made from
  1 pint Jersey (U.S. 2½ cups) milk (see page 112)
6 oz. paneer, made from
  2 pints (U.S. 5 cups) Jersey milk (see page 89)
2 oz. flour
pinch bicarbonate of soda
oil for deep frying

Make the syrup by dissolving the sugar in the water over gentle heat. Then boil rapidly for five minutes. Set aside to cool. Put the khoa and paneer into a large bowl. Wet palms of hands and knead the mixture until quite smooth. Then add the sieved flour and bicarbonate of soda and continue to knead for another 15—20 minutes. Set aside for 15 minutes. Divide and mould dough into walnut-sized balls and deep fry till golden brown then drain. Add rose water to the syrup. Soak the sweets in the syrup for at least 4 hours before serving.

Milk sweets in syrup

the milk and return to heat. Stir to dissolve sugar and cook till mixture becomes creamy. Add the crushed cardamom seeds. Serve cold.

GOBI KHEER

CAULIFLOWER SWEET

Preparation time   5 minutes
Cooking time   1 hour
To serve   4

You will need

2 pints (U.S. 5 cups) Jersey milk
8 oz. cauliflower
2 oz. unsalted butter
4-6 oz. sugar
8 cardamom seeds, peeled and crushed

TO DECORATE

  few cloves

Bring milk to the boil in a large, heavy pan. Lower heat and cook till milk begins to thicken (about 45 minutes). Trim the cauliflour and finely chop flowerets. Melt butter in a pan and fry the cauliflower until brown. Add cauliflower and sugar to

SUJI BARFI

SEMOLINA SWEET

Preparation time   5 minutes
Cooking time   15 minutes
To serve   4

You will need

4 oz. semolina
1 lb. sugar
1½ pints milk
4 oz. unsalted butter
vanilla essence *or*
  6 cardamon seeds crushed

TO DECORATE

chopped nuts
silver leaves

Mix the semolina and sugar in a large saucepan. Slowly mix in milk and melted butter. Bring to the boil then reduce the heat and cook very gently, stirring constantly, till mixture becomes very thick. Add flavouring and continue to cook till mixture leaves the sides of the pan. Spread it in a shallow, greased dish and flatten to ½-inch thickness. Cool and cut into squares. Decorate with chopped nuts and silver leaves.

KADU HALWA

MARROW PUDDING

Preparation time 10 minutes
Cooking time 1½ hours
To serve 4

You will need

1 lb. marrow
1-2 tablespoons water
6 oz. khoa, made from
    2 pints (U.S. 5 cups) Jersey milk (see page 139)
4 oz. sugar
2 oz. unsalted butter
1 oz. almonds, flaked
2 tablespoons raisins
½ teaspoon grated nutmeg

Peel, de-seed and finely chop the marrow. Put in a pan with 1—2 tablespoons of water. Simmer until all liquid is absorbed and the marrow soft. Add the khoa, sugar and butter and cook till the mixture comes away from the sides of the pan. Add the almonds and raisins. Put in a dish, sprinkle with nutmeg and serve cold.

JALLEBI

BATTER SWEETS IN SYRUP

Preparation time 10 minutes
Cooking time 20 minutes
To serve 4

You will need

8 oz. flour
¼ oz. yeast, dissolved in
    ½ tablespoon warm water
½ teaspoon saffron, soaked in
    1 tablespoon hot water
1½ tablespoons yoghurt
8 oz. sugar
½ pint (U.S. 1¼ cups) water
2 cardamom seeds
oil for deep frying

Sieve flour into a bowl. Add the yeast, water strained from the saffron and the yoghurt. Mix well

adding water if necessary to make a batter the consistency of thick cream. Cover and set aside for 2 hours.
Dissolve the sugar in the water, over gentle heat. Bring to the boil and continue to boil rapidly until a thick syrup is formed. Add the peeled cardamoms. Heat the oil. Put the batter into a forcing bag fitted with an ⅛-inch plain nozzle and pipe figures of eight and rings into the hot oil. When set turn over and fry to a pale golden colour. Drain, soak in the syrup for 2—3 minutes. Drain and serve.

BOMBAY HALWA

CORNFLOUR DESSERT

Preparation time 10 minutes
Cooking time 40-50 minutes
To serve 4

You will need

8 oz. sugar
½ pint (U.S. 1¼ cups) plus 4 tablespoons water
2 tablespoons cornflour
few drops of food colouring
2 teaspoons lemon juice
2 oz. unsalted butter
1 tablespoon almonds, sliced
1 tablespoon *each* cashew nuts and
    ·pistachios, chopped
½ teaspoon crushed cardamom seeds

Put sugar with ½ pint (U.S. 1¼ cups) water into a pan. Dissolve sugar on a low heat. When completely dissolved bring to the boil and boil for five minutes. Meanwhile mix the cornflour with the remaining water till smooth. Take the syrup off the heat and when it has stopped bubbling add the cornflour and return to the heat. Add colouring (green, red or yellow are the traditional colours) and cook, stirring continuosly till the mixture solidifies. Mix in the lemon juice. Add the butter a little at a time, stirring all the time till all butter is absorbed. Keep on cooking till mixture separates from the side of the pan. Mix in the nuts and cardamoms. Spread in a shallow dish and flatten out with a knife. Cool and when completely set, cut into squares with a sharp knife.

Curried meat with spinach

Brain curry

BASOONDI

CREAMY DESSERT

Preparation time 5 minutes
Cooking time 1 hour
To serve 4

You will need

3 pints (U.S. 7½ cups) Jersey milk
4 oz. sugar
½ teaspoon grated nutmeg
1 oz. almonds, blanched
1 oz. pistachio nuts

Boil milk rapidly in a heavy saucepan, stirring all the time, till reduced to 1 pint (U.S. 2½ cups). This takes approximately 1 hour. Add sugar, stir to dissolve and cook for a few more minutes. Remove from the heat and allow to cool. Add nutmeg, stir and pour into a serving dish, scraping cream from sides of the pan. Coarsely grate the nuts and sprinkle on top. Serve chilled.

KHEER

RICE PUDDING

Preparation time 5 minutes
Cooking time 1½ hours
To serve 4

You will need

2 oz. Patna or Basmati rice
2 pints (U.S. 5 cups) milk
4 oz. sugar
pinch of salt
1 oz. raisins
½ teaspoon grated nutmeg *or*
 1 teaspoon cardamom seeds, crushed

Wash the rice thoroughly and put with the milk in a heavy pan and simmer on a low heat for 1½ hours. Stir frequently and mash the rice with the back of the spoon. When it is the consistency of thick cream add the sugar, salt and raisins. Cook for a few more minutes till the mixture thickens again to a creamy consistency. Take off the heat and add the flavouring. Serve cold in small bowls.

COCONUT MANGO FOOL

Preparation time 30 minutes
To serve 4

You will need

6 mangoes
4 tablespoons desiccated coconut, soaked in
 ½ pint (U.S. 1¼ cups) hot milk
sugar to taste
½ teaspoon ground cardamom seeds
pinch of saffron powder
18 almonds, shredded
pinch of salt

Peel mangoes, chop and pass through a coarse sieve. Strain coconut milk, discard the pulp and add the milk to the mango. Add sugar and stir till dissolved. Add cardamom, saffron, almonds and salt. Chill and serve with whipped cream.

BELLANA

RICE AND MOLASSES PUDDING

Cooking time 30 minutes
To serve 4

You will need

4 oz. Patna rice
2 tablespoons mollasses
1 tablespoon water
1 oz. fried cashew nuts
1 teaspoon cardamom seeds, crushed
2 tablespoon sesame seeds, fried and crushed
1 oz. unsalted butter
2 oz. grated fresh *or*
 desiccated coconut.

Boil rice and set aside. Heat the mollasses with the water over gentle heat. Add cashew nuts, cardamon, sesame and a knob of the butter. Stir well and add the rice. Cook gently, stirring constantly for about 25 minutes. Add coconut and remaining butter. Stir and cook for a further three minutes. Remove from heat and serve hot.

GULAB CHAWAL

ROSE FLAVOURED RICE

Preparation time 20 minutes
Cooking time 1 hour
To serve 4

You will need

* 1 lb. fresh rose petals
¾ pint (U.S. 2 cups) water
8 oz. Patna rice
¼ pint (U.S. ⅔ cup) double cream
1½ oz. sugar
1 tablespoon shredded almonds

---

* When roses are not in bloom add 1 dessertspoon of rose water.

Tie rose petals in two muslin bags. Boil a scant ½ pint (U.S. 1¼ cups) of the water in a saucepan and place petals in it. Take off the heat, cover with a lid. Boil cleaned rice in the remaining water and when the water is absorbed, put the rice in an ovenproof dish. Remove the rose petals from the syrup without squeezing the bags. Add the scented water to the rice. Put the rice in a moderate oven (350° F. — Gas Mark 4) and bake till the rice is cooked. Beat the cream and add with the sugar and almonds to the rice. Chill before serving.

SEVIAN

VERMICELLI PUDDING

Preparation time 5 minutes
Cooking time 30—40 minutes
To serve 4

You will need

3 oz. unsalted butter
6 oz. vermicelli
8 oz. sugar
¾ pint (U.S. 2 cups) milk
pinch of saffron powder
6 crushed cardamom seeds

TO DECORATE

1 oz. shredded almonds

Heat butter in a saucepan and fry the vermicelli until golden brown — be careful not to burn it. Pour in the milk, bring to the boil, lower the heat and simmer, covered, till vermicelli is cooked. Stir occasionally to prevent sticking. Uncover and cook till the milk evaporates. Add sugar and cook uncovered till dry, stirring continuously. Add cardamom and saffron. Serve on a plate garnished with shredded almonds.

MALPURA

SWEET PANCAKES

Preparation time 10 minutes
Cooking time 20 minutes
To serve 4

You will need

5 oz. semolina
pinch bicarbonate of soda
4 oz. plain flour
5 oz. sugar
pinch ground cardamom seeds
pinch of saffron
½–¾ pint (U.S. 1¼–2 cups) butter milk
ghee or oil for frying

Rice flour pudding

Reserve 2 tablespoons semolina and the bicarbonate of soda. In a large mixing bowl combine the remaining dry ingredients and mix to a batter with the buttermilk. Set aside overnight. The following day add the reserved semolina and bicarbonate of soda. Shallow fry the mixture in ghee, or oil, by dropping a tablespoonful at a time into the pan. Turn once during cooking. The edges of the pancakes should be crisp and brown but the centre should remain soft. Drain and serve hot.

PHIRNI

RICE FLOUR PUDDING

Cooking time   35-40 minutes
To serve   4

You will need

1½ pints (U.S. 3¾ cups) milk
1½ oz. rice flour
4 oz. sugar
1 teaspoon rose water
½ oz. each almonds *and*
    pistachios blanched and shredded
1 dessertspoon raisins

TO DECORATE

blanched almonds

Almond sweet

Bring milk to boil. Add rice flour and cook gently on a medium heat stirring frequently, till mixture thickens to creamy consistency. Add sugar dissolve and cook till mixture thickens again. Cool, add rose water, raisins and pistachios. Serve in a bowl or individual glasses. Decorate with the almonds.

BADAM BARFI

ALMOND AND MILK TOFFEE

Cooking time   1 hour 20 minutes
To serve   4

You will need

2 pints (U.S. 5 cups) Jersey milk
4 oz. ground almonds
3 oz. sugar
½ teaspoon crushed cardamom seeds

Make khoa from the milk following the recipe on page 139. When on the point of setting add the almonds and sugar. Mix well and continue cooking till the mixture comes away from the sides of the pan. Stir continuously. Spread the toffee into a shallow, greased tin. Sprinkle with the crushed cardamom. Cool before cutting into squares.

PUDINA KA SHERBET

MINT DRINK

Preparation time   5 minutes
To serve   4

You will need

small bunch mint leaves
1 tablespoon aniseed
4 tablespoons sugar
2 pints (U.S. 5 cups) water

Crush mint leaves and aniseed. Put sugar and water in a pan on gentle heat. Dissolve sugar then bring to the boil and boil for one minute. Pour boiling syrup over mint and aniseed and leave, covered, to infuse for one hour. Chill and serve.

BADAM HALWA

ALMOND SWEET

Preparation time 5 minutes
Cooking time 30 minutes
To serve 4

You will need

6 oz. sugar
5 tablespoons water
pinch saffron
4 oz. ground almonds
4 oz. unsalted butter
6 ground cardamom seeds

Dissolve the sugar in the water over low heat then bring to the boil. Boil to 220°F. or soft ball. Lower heat and add saffron and almonds. Gradually add the butter, stirring continuously. When the mixture thickens pour into a shallow, greased dish and sprinkle the top with the crushed cardamom. Allow to cool and cut into squares.

GAJJAR KHEER

CARROT PUDDING

Preparation time 15 minutes
Cooking time 1 hour
To serve 4

You will need

12 oz. carrots
2 pints (U.S. 5 cups) Jersey milk
6 oz. sugar
6 cardamom seeds

FOR DECORATION

almonds and raisins

Wash, peel and grate carrots. Boil the milk for about 30 minutes till reduced by half. Add the carrots and cook till mixture thickens. Add the sugar and crushed cardamoms and continue to cook till thick. Decorate with chopped nuts and raisins. Serve hot or cold.

MYSORE PAK

GRAM FLOUR SWEET

Preparation time 5 minutes
Cooking time 25 minutes
To serve 4

You will need

6 oz. sugar
3 oz. water
8 oz. unsalted butter
3 oz. gram flour
½ teaspoon grated nutmeg

Prepare a syrup by dissolving then boiling the sugar in the water for three minutes. Meanwhile, heat 2 oz. butter in a frying pan and add the sifted gram flour. Fry for two minutes stirring constantly. Add the syrup and continue to cook, stirring all the time for three minutes. Now add the rest of the butter, a small piece at a time, letting each piece be absorbed before adding the next. Cook gently until the mixture begins to fall away from the sides of the pan — about 15 minutes. Be careful not to burn. Pour into a flat, greased tin, sprinkle with nutmeg and leave to set. Cut into squares or diamond shapes before it becomes completely cool.

DOODH SHERBET

MILK DRINK

Preparation time 15 minutes
Cooking time 35 minutes
To serve 4

You will need

2 pints (U.S. 5 cups) milk
4 oz. sugar
¼ pint (U.S. ⅔ cup) water
2 teaspoons rose water
2 oz. almonds
2 oz. pistachios
pinch crushed cardamom seeds
pinch of saffron powder

Put milk in a heavy pan and cook for 30 minutes to reduce by half. Make a syrup by dissolving sugar in water and then boiling for five minutes. Allow both milk and syrup to cool. When quite cool, sieve or liquidise in a blender with nuts and flavouring. When smooth, chill and serve.

KELA HALWA

BANANA SWEET

Preparation time   10 minutes
Cooking time   1 hour
To serve   4

You will need

5 large bananas
6 oz. sugar
½ pint (U.S. 1¼ cups) water
4 oz. unsalted butter
1 teaspoon ground cardamom seeds

TO DECORATE

chopped seedless raisins

Skin and mash the bananas. Add sugar and water and cook with butter, stirring constantly, until the mixture begins to thicken. Remove the pan from the heat and test by cooling a little of the mixture on a plate. If it can be stretched it is cooked. Mix the cardamoms into the bananas. Spread on a greas-ed, shallow, tin and cool for 15 minutes. Then cut into squares. Decorate with chopped raisins.

NARIEL BARFI

COCONUT MILK TOFFEE

Preparation time   5 minutes
Cooking time   1 hour
To serve   4

You will need

2 pints (U.S. 5 cups) milk
4 oz. desiccated or freshly grated coconut
3 oz. granulated sugar
few drops of pink colouring
1 teaspoon rose water *or*
   10 cardamom seeds, crushed

Bring the milk to the boil in a heavy pan and cook briskly stirring constantly until reduced by half — approximately 30 minutes. Then add the coconut and sugar and continue cooking and stirring until very thick. Add the colouring and flavouring and turn into a shallow, greased tin. Cool and cut into squares.

INDEX

151

ACKNOWLEDGEMENTS

The Author and Publishers would like to thank:

Mr. Sadia of the Tandoori Restaurant, 153, Fulham Road, London,
S.W.3. for the use of the premises and for providing facilities,
enabling us to produce the photographs in this book.

They would also like to thank Indiacraft Limited for the loan
of properties used in these pictures.